Lata Mangeshkar: My Favourites, Vol. 2

33 1/3 Global

33 1/3 Global, a series related to but independent from **33 1/3**, takes the format of the original series of short, music-based books and brings the focus to music throughout the world. With initial volumes focusing on Japanese and Brazilian music, the series will also include volumes on the popular music of Australia/Oceania, Europe, Africa, the Middle East, and more.

33 1/3 Japan

Series Editor: Noriko Manabe

Spanning a range of artists and genres—from the 1970s rock of Happy End to technopop band Yellow Magic Orchestra, the Shibuya-kei of Cornelius, classic anime series *Cowboy Bebop*, J-Pop/EDM hybrid Perfume, and vocaloid star Hatsune Miku—**33 1/3 Japan** is a series devoted to in-depth examination of Japanese popular music of the twentieth and twenty-first centuries.

Published Titles:
Supercell's *Supercell* by Keisuke Yamada
AKB48 by Patrick W. Galbraith and Jason G. Karlin
Yoko Kanno's *Cowboy Bebop Soundtrack* by Rose Bridges
Perfume's *Game* by Patrick St. Michel
Cornelius's *Fantasma* by Martin Roberts
Joe Hisaishi's *My Neighbor Totoro: Soundtrack* by Kunio Hara
Shonen Knife's *Happy Hour* by Brooke McCorkle
Nenes' *Koza Dabasa* by Henry Johnson
Yuming's *The 14th Moon* by Lasse Lehtonen
Toshiko Akiyoshi-Lew Tabackin Big Band's *Kogun* by E. Taylor Atkins

Forthcoming Titles:
Yellow Magic Orchestra's *Yellow Magic Orchestra* by Toshiyuki Ohwada
Kohaku utagassen: The Red and White Song Contest by Shelley Brunt
S.O.B.'s *Don't Be Swindle* by Mahon Murphy and Ran Zwigenberg

33 1/3 Brazil

Series Editor: Jason Stanyek

Covering the genres of samba, tropicália, rock, hip hop, forró, bossa nova, heavy metal and funk, among others, **33 1/3 Brazil** is a series devoted to in-depth examination of the most important Brazilian albums of the twentieth and twenty-first centuries.

Published Titles:

Caetano Veloso's *A Foreign Sound* by Barbara Browning
Tim Maia's *Tim Maia Racional Vols. 1 &2* by Allen Thayer
João Gilberto and Stan Getz's *Getz/Gilberto* by Brian McCann
Gilberto Gil's *Refazenda* by Marc A. Hertzman
Dona Ivone Lara's *Sorriso Negro* by Mila Burns
Milton Nascimento and Lô Borges's *The Corner Club* by Jonathon Grasse
Racionais MCs' *Sobrevivendo no Inferno* by Derek Pardue
Naná Vasconcelos's *Saudades* by Daniel B. Sharp
Chico Buarque's First *Chico Buarque* by Charles A. Perrone

Forthcoming titles:

Jorge Ben Jor's *África Brasil* by Frederick J. Moehn

33 1/3 Europe

Series Editor: Fabian Holt

Spanning a range of artists and genres, 33 1/3 Europe offers engaging accounts of popular and culturally significant albums of Continental Europe and the North Atlantic from the twentieth and twenty-first centuries.

Published Titles:

Darkthrone's *A Blaze in the Northern Sky* by Ross Hagen
Ivo Papazov's *Balkanology* by Carol Silverman
Heiner Müller and Heiner Goebbels's *Wolokolamsker Chaussee* by Philip V. Bohlman
Modeselektor's *Happy Birthday!* by Sean Nye

Mercyful Fate's *Don't Break the Oath* by Henrik Marstal
Bea Playa's *I'll Be Your Plaything* by Anna Szemere and András Rónai
Various Artists' *DJs do Guetto* by Richard Elliott
Czesław Niemen's *Niemen Enigmatic* by Ewa Mazierska and Mariusz Gradowski
Massada's *Astaganaga* by Lutgard Mutsaers
Los Rodriguez's *Sin Documentos* by Fernán del Val and Héctor Fouce
Édith Piaf's *Récital 1961* by David Looseley
Nuovo Canzoniere Italiano's *Bella Ciao* by Jacopo Tomatis
Iannis Xenakis's *Persepolis* by Aram Yardumian
Vopli Vidopliassova's *Tantsi* by Maria Sonevytsky
Amália Rodrigues's *Amália at the Olympia* by Lila Ellen Gray
Ardit Gjebrea's *Projekt Jon* by Nicholas Tochka
Aqua's *Aquarium* by C.C. McKee
Einstürzende Neubauten's *Kollaps* by Melle Jan Kromhout and Jan Nieuwenhuis
J.M.K.E.'s *To the Cold Land* by Brigitta Davidjants

Forthcoming Titles:
Taco Hemingway's *Jarmark* by Kamila Rymajdo
Tripes' *Kefali Gemato Hrisafi* by Dafni Tragaki
Silly's *Februar* by Michael Rauhut
CCCP's *Fedeli Alla Linea's 1964-1985 Affinità-Divergenze Fra Il Compagno Togliatti E Noi Del Conseguimento Della Maggiore Età* by Giacomo Bottà
Sigur Rós' *Ágætis Byrjun* by Tore Størvold

33 1/3 Oceania

Series Editors: Jon Stratton (senior editor) and Jon Dale (specializing in books on albums from Aotearoa/New Zealand)
Spanning a range of artists and genres from Australian Indigenous artists to Maori and Pasifika artists, from Aotearoa/New Zealand noise music to Australian rock, and including music from Papua and other Pacific islands, **33 1/3 Oceania** offers exciting accounts of albums that illustrate the wide range of music made in the Oceania region.

Published Titles:

John Farnham's *Whispering Jack* by Graeme Turner

The Church's *Starfish* by Chris Gibson

Regurgitator's *Unit* by Lachlan Goold and Lauren Istvandity

Kylie Minogue's *Kylie* by Adrian Renzo and Liz Giuffre

Alastair Riddell's *Space Waltz* by Ian Chapman

Hunters & Collectors's *Human Frailty* by Jon Stratton

The Front Lawn's *Songs from the Front Lawn* by Matthew Bannister

Bic Runga's *Drive* by Henry Johnson

The Dead C's *Clyma est mort* by Darren Jorgensen

Ed Kuepper's *Honey Steel's Gold* by John Encarnacao

Chain's *Toward the Blues* by Peter Beilharz

Hilltop Hoods' *The Calling* by Dianne Rodger

Screamfeeder's *Kitten Licks* by Ben Green and Ian Rogers

Soundtrack from *Saturday Night Fever* by Clinton Walker

Forthcoming Titles:

The Triffids' *Born Sandy Devotional* by Christina Ballico

Crowded House's *Together Alone* by Barnaby Smith

5MMM's *Compilation Album of Adelaide Bands 1980* by Collette Snowden

The Clean's *Boodle Boodle Boodle* by Geoff Stahl

INXS' *Kick* by Ryan Daniel and Lauren Moxey

Sunnyboys' *Sunnyboys* by Stephen Bruel

Eyeliner's *Buy Now* by Michael Brown

Silverchair's *Frogstomp* by Jay Daniel Thompson

TISM's *Machiavelli and the Four Seasons* by Tyler Jenke

The La De Das' *The Happy Prince* by John Tebbutt

John Sangster's *Lord of the Rings, Vols. 1–3* by Bruce Johnson

Gary Shearston's *Dingo* by Peter Mills

The Avalanches' *Since I Left You* by Charles Fairchild

Kate Ceberano's *Brave* by Panizza Allmark

Robert Forster's *Danger in the Past* by Patrick Chapman

Various Artists' *A Truckload of Sky: The Lost Songs of David McComb* by Glenn D'Cruz

33 1/3 South Asia

Series Editor: Natalie Sarrazin

From the films of Bollywood and Lollywood, to home-grown *bhangra* hip-hop, Hindu devotional pop and Sufi rock, Sri Lankan rap, Indo jazz and disco, new-wave electronica and diasporic Asian Underground scene, **33 1/3 South Asia** takes readers on a sonically diverse journey through the most significant soundtracks and albums from the twentieth and twenty-first centuries.

Published:

Dil Chahta Hai Soundtrack by Jayson Beaster-Jones

Lata Mangeshkar: *My Favourites, Volume 2* by Anirudha Bhattacharjee and Chandrashekhar Rao

Forthcoming:

Coke Studio (Season 14) by Rakae Rehman Jamil and Khadija Muzaffar

Lata Mangeshkar: My Favourites, Vol. 2

Anirudha Bhattacharjee and
Chandrashekhar Rao

33 1/3 SOUTH ASIA

Series Editor: Natalie Sarrazin

BLOOMSBURY
NEW DELHI • LONDON • OXFORD • NEW YORK • SYDNEY

BLOOMSBURY INDIA
Bloomsbury Publishing India Pvt. Ltd
Second Floor, LSC Building No. 4, DDA Complex, Pocket C–6&7,
Vasant Kunj, New Delhi 110070

BLOOMSBURY, Bloomsbury Academic India and the Diana
logo are trademarks of Bloomsbury Publishing Plc

First published in India 2025
First published in the United States of America 2025

British Library Cataloguing-in-Publication Data
A catalogue record for this book is available from the British Library

Library of Congress Cataloging-in-Publication Data
A catalog record for this book is available from the Library of Congress

ISBN: 978-93-61312-77-9

Typeset by Deanta Global Publishing Services, Chennai, India
Typeset by Integra Software services Pvt. Ltdz

Printed in India by Manipal Technologies Limited, Manipal

To find out more about our authors and books visit
www.bloomsbury.com and sign up for our newsletters.

Contents

Who is Lata Mangeshkar? xi
Lata Mangeshkar and LP records: A story xiv
Documenting the album xvii
Nomenclature and sources used in the book xix
Getting started xxii
Music Director xxii
Lyricist xxv

1 **In the beginning** 1
Master Ghulam Haider – the melody queen maker 1
Masterji – Khemchand Prakash 4
Anil Biswas – the first star 6

2 **The trailblazers** 11
Shankar Jaikishan – the allrounders 11

3 **The classicists** 23
Naushad – the 'Lucknavi' master 23
Sachin Dev Burman – the folkman from Bengal 26
Roshan – ode to Hindustani classical 31
Jaidev – the fakir 34

4 **The conventional** 39
Husnlal Bhagatram – The sound of Punjab 39
Shyam Sundar – pathos of Punjab 41
Vasant Desai – soft and colourful 43

5 **The unconventional** 49

C. Ramchandra – music is fun 49

Salil Chowdhury – the genius 52

Sajjad Hussain – the perfectionist 57

6 **The tearful craving** 61

Madan Mohan – closest to the heart 61

7 **The trailblazers – II** 69

Rahul Dev Burman – the modernist 69

Laxmikant Pyarelal – the born survivors 76

8 **The subdued nuances** 83

Hemant Kumar – friendly notes 83

Khayyam – poetic feel 86

Rajesh Roshan – relaxed gait 91

Ghulam Mohammed – pure heart 94

9 **The less spoken** 99

Chitragupta – the gentle soul 99

S. Mohinder – solitary reaper 103

10 **The lesser heard** 107

Hridaynath Mangeshkar – family 108

Fayyaz Shaukat and K. Mahavir – lesser knowns 111

11 **The last song** 115

Ravindra Jain – Raj Kapoor's last magnum opus 115

12 **Summing up** 117

Acknowledgements 119

Index 121

Who is Lata Mangeshkar?

The opportunity to write about India's best-known singer was both exciting and challenging. Almost her entire body of work is now accessible, as are numerous analyses by musicologists and other authors. Yet, most listeners in India that the authors interacted with are unable to recall when and where they first heard her; we have all arrived sometime in the middle because she has always been there (an emotion she inspires even in her nonagenarian fans). It was at no particular moment that she entered our lives.

Yet she remains a nebulous and ethereal presence; a diffuse, misty haze. Like the nuns sang of Maria Von Trapp, 'How do you hold a moonbeam in your hand?'

Of course, there is no other-worldly explanation. There cannot be.

If one were to try and analyse this logically, credit must be given not only to a lengthy career spanning seven-odd decades, a colossal and eclectic output of songs traversing all emotions and script situations, but also to the paramount role played by the film song per se in the psyche of the Indian listener.

Unlike Hollywood, where a 'musical' is simply another genre, in India almost *all* films are musical by default. When you consider that every film has about six songs and that an average of 1,500–2,000 films (in around twenty languages, including Hindi) are released every year – that's a *lot* of songs! The nostalgia inspired by these songs isn't limited to memories of watching the film, the particular situation in the film where the song appeared, of the actor or actress who lip-synced it on screen, its tune or its lyrics, or even of Lata's rendition (this would be true of any other 'playback' artiste, as lip-syncing singers are called in India) – it fans out to encompass which cinema and in which city we saw it, and with whom – and that's a *lot* of memories too. As Asha Bhosle (Lata's equally preeminent singing sister) once remarked, 'All the songs we remember so fondly are like many houses we once lived in'.

Again, unlike in the West, where the original composer/writer retains the moral right to assert copyright and thereby allows for any number of singers to perform their work as a 'cover version' after giving them due credit and royalties, few tend to think of an Indian film song sung by Lata as a team effort – it is first and foremost a 'Lata song'; such is her overwhelming and lasting impact.

There have been attempts to re-record cover versions of her songs too by another playback singer. A peculiar trait of Indian film songs explains the failure of these to gel with the public. Film song addicts like to hear their favourites exactly as originally recorded, whether rendered by another singer or even by the original singer in a different setting (for instance, in a live performance). As playback singer Manna Dey explains why Lata's concerts are so successful: 'She reproduces every syllable, phrase, comma and semicolon just as in the original'.

Consequently, even if another cover artiste attempts this kind of exactness, nobody can be more exact than the original, right?

She led a long life well into her 90s, and that helped too. Her earliest listeners (who could ill afford to buy records on a regular basis or a gramophone to play them on, or visit the movies multiple times to hear a song again) had to be content with tinny reproductions played over a radio (with short-wave reception further diminishing the clarity), but fans of subsequent generations managed to build up collections during the cassette tape and CD era, and today, thanks to technology and ardent archivists, are now able to revisit her songs, even of the 1940s and 1950s, in excellent clarity, courtesy of the generosity of YouTube uploaders. Lata Mangeshkar lived and worked through all these times, which explains further the impression of perpetuity she conveys.

Lata Mangeshkar and LP records: A story

Lata Mangeshkar – My Favourites Volume 2 (also referred to as *Volume 2* or *LM – Vol 2* in subsequent mentions) is a compilation of fifty Hindi songs spread over a period of forty years. This collection of four long-playing records (LPs) was packaged as a product in 1988 by HMV (His Masters Voice), with the album numbers being PMLP 1221/22/23/24. A corresponding set of four cassettes was also released at the same time. Forty-six of the fifty were songs from feature films. The rest were initially released as part of non-film song compilations. As the name suggests, Lata Mangeshkar (28 September 1929 to 6 February 2022) sang all the songs, in whole as solos or in parts as duets.

The tradition of compiling an assortment of Hindi films' songs in the form of LPs started in the 1950s. The first well-known of such attempts was *Modern Motion Picture Music of India* by the Gramophone Company of India (GCI) in 1957. The disc contained twelve songs, six on each side, sung by Lata Mangeshkar and/or Hemanta Kumar Mukherjee (aka Hemant Kumar) for *Anarkali* (1953) and *Nagin* (1954), both films produced by Filmistan Limited, Bombay (now Mumbai). The first Lata Mangeshkar LP to receive nationwide popularity was *Haunting Melodies of Lata Mangeshkar* in 1967, produced by GCI.

Lata Mangeshkar enacted a paramount role in the propagation of film soundtracks through LPs. The 12″-diameter LPs that played at 33.3 rpm were invented in the 1950s, but it took another decade for Hindi film soundtracks to be issued regularly in this format. Unlike the earlier brittle 78s that were restricted to around three-and-a-half minutes' playing time on each side, vinyl LPs were more durable and had a playing time of twenty-two minutes per side. With their handsome and colourful jacket covers featuring photographs of the film's stars, detailed sleeve notes and all songs in full (including the lesser-heard third stanza that one would otherwise get to hear only in the film if included), LPs soon became coveted by the select few who could afford them.

But it wasn't only for music-loving customers that an LP became a status symbol. Film producers too wanted a glossy LP issued of their upcoming films – it lent a touch of class to the production and evoked the image that theirs was a Grade A movie. It could well be inferred that releasing an LP became a well-respected metric of social currency, a status symbol. Consequently, many companies set up LP manufacturing and distribution units in India, but much of the market share belonged to GCI, which held a stranglehold monopoly until the advent of Polydor in 1970 with *The Train* (1970), but that label remained a distant second. Hence, every film producer was eager to sign a deal with GCI to sell their music in the form of LP records.

There was only one catch. It had to be approved by Vijay Kishore Dubey (?–2010), music producer and boss of the monopolistic Gramophone Company of India's HMV arm. And what would be his chief yardstick to determine saleability? Lata Mangeshkar.

Mr Dubey would scrutinize the aspiring film's song listing, and only if the soundtrack featured Lata predominantly would it get a stamp of approval. Sure, there was no problem with the choice of male singer (if his tracks did not outnumber hers), but other female singers, even her sister Asha Bhosle (born 1933), had to make do with a single token vamp-type song. If, for the producer, getting that LP made was paramount, some Lata songs would need to be added or redone in her voice – or else it was back to the good old 78 rpm shellacs or (at most) a four-song vinyl EP. Mr Dubey may well have been right!

Simultaneously, the business of compilation LPs became very popular. Given its vast repository of songs, this developed into a key bread earner for GCI, and gradually for other music companies as well.

Documenting the album

Volume 2 happened post the huge success of the first volume with the same name in 1987. It was conceived after Ms Mangeshkar received requests – both verbal and in the form of mail – to list a second collection. Consequently, this became the only compilation where Lata personally identified the songs as her 'Favourites'. She authenticated the same with three short commentaries, one before the first song, one midway through the album and another after the last song, splitting the album into two distinct parts.

Devising a method to write about the album was an arduous task, in the sense that there was no guideline on how and why Lata chose the songs. This was like any other compilation from her oeuvre of approximately 5,781 Hindi songs.[1] Handicapped, and in the absence of a concrete structure except chronology, we used her commentary to our advantage, where she said,

> *Before stepping into the path of music, I had received some basic musical education from my revered father. I had fondly listened to the singers of early film music whose tunes kept resonating in my soul, and whose voice had entered my mind. My songs are the flowers of my devotion towards them. Looking back, I find that my journey of music would not have started if many kind and famous music directors had not given me an opportunity. I remember*

them with reverence. Furthermore, they guided me on the way to a musical career.

In view of Lata's own admission, we thought that this was an opportunity to arrange the songs composer wise, fitting the music makers in a genre they broadly represented, while also respecting the timeline. For example, the masters who shaped her initial period have been clubbed under the chapter 'In the beginning'. Composers who broadly followed the tenets of Hindustani classical and folk music are covered under 'The Classicists'. The categorizations are self-explanatory and would help the reader in appreciating the multiple aspects of Hindi film and non-film music. It is to be noted that more than 95 per cent (5,524songs)[2] of her Hindi output is for the cinema, hence, the non-film songs that have been included in the album are clubbed together for better comprehension of the segment. The chronological angle used might help to generate interest regarding the history of Hindi cinema as well.

Notes

1 Snehasis Chatterjee, *Meri Awaaz Hi Pehchan Hai – Discography of Songs Sung by Lata Mangeshkar, Volume 2,* page 605.

2 Ibid.

Nomenclature and sources used in the book

1. Italics have been used for films names when used part of the main text (as per house rules, song names are within inverted commas).
2. Acronyms have been used for film names when repeated. For example, *BKR* for *Barsaat ki Raat*. Similar nomenclature has been used for people, for example, SD for Sachin Dev Burman. For composers who operated in pairs, their names have been shortened using initials separated by a hyphen, for example, L-P for Laxmikant Pyarelal, and so on.
3. Film names are supplemented with the censor year in brackets the first time they are used in the book.
4. In Hindustani classical music,
   - **a.** Thaat is the equivalent of a scale in Western music.
   - **b.** Raag is a phrase using a set of fixed notes (mostly).
   - **c.** Murki is a fast and delicate ornamentation.

d. Harkat is a variation to a phrase that is repeated in a song.

e. Dhun is a short phrase, mostly instrumental, but could also be sung.

f. Taan is a fast phrase mostly sung at the end of a song.

g. Taal is the equivalent of rhythm. These are broken into time signatures like 4/4, 3/4, 7/4 and so on, and have specific names like Keharba, Khemta, Addha, Teentaal, Dadra, Rupak, Tewra, Jhaptaal, Deepchandi and so forth, based on the notes of the Indian drums (pakhavaj, tabla).

5. Songs in Hindi or Hindustani music are divided into four parts:

   a. Asthayi or Mukhra (the first two lines that get repeated)

   b. Antara (phrase that comes after the asthayi)

   c. Sanchari (an additional phrase in a different tune, that appears before one of the antaras)

   d. Abhog (equivalent of a coda in Western music).

6. Shayari is an independent phrase, sometimes recited rather than sung, before the asthayi.

7. Generally, Hindi film songs have an asthayi and two or more antaras. Sanchari and Abhog are rare. Shayari is used sporadically.

8. For people who are no more, we have tried to give their years of birth and death from what is available.

For those living, we have avoided giving the year of birth. The exceptions are her co-singers, lyricists and composers.

9. Song statistics have been sourced from Snehasis Chatterjee's *Meri Awaaz Hi Pehchan Hai*, which contains the list of all the songs recorded by Lata Mangeshkar with their disc numbers.
10. Song-raag mapping has been mostly sourced from musicologist Kanhaya Lal Pandey and his book *Hindi Cine Raag Encyclopedia Volume 1&2* (Lucknow: Sangeet Shilp Prakashan, 2020).
11. As our stories go back in time, we have tried to stick to names like Bombay, Calcutta and Madras, and not Mumbai, Kolkata and Chennai, respectively, unless an interview was conducted later or the names have been used by the publishers of the books referenced.
12. We have used terms 'actor' and 'actress' to help the reader identify with the gender.
13. The translations from Hindi are by the authors unless mentioned otherwise.

Getting started

To help the readers get acquainted with the names and their impact in terms of volume in the Hindi music industry, here are some numbers related to the music directors and the lyricists whose work form part of *LM – Vol 2*.

Music Director

Name	Period Active as a Composer of Hindi Songs	Number of Songs for Lata Mangeshkar	Number of Songs in the Collection
Anil Biswas (1914–2003)	1932–65	129	2
C. Ramchandra (1918–82)	1935–71	303	1
Chitragupta Srivastava (1917–91)	1946–88	265	2
Fayyaz Ahmed Khan (1924–87)	Fleeting	2	1
Ghulam Haider (1908–53)	1932–53	9	1
Ghulam Mohammed (1903–68)	1931–68	79	1

Name	Period Active as a Composer of Hindi Songs	Number of Songs for Lata Mangeshkar	Number of Songs in the Collection
Hemanta Kumar Mukherjee (1920–89)	1935–79	185	1
Hridaynath Mangeshkar (born 1937)	1955–present	261	3
Husnlal (1920–1968) Bhagatram (1914–73)	1930s–late 1960s	106	1
Jaidev Verma (1918–87)	1955–87	37	2
K. Mahavir (?–1987)	?–1987	4	1
Khayyam (1927–2019)	1948–2016	76	3
Khemchand Prakash (1907–50)	1935–50	15	1
Laxmikant Kudalkar (1937–98) Pyarelal Sharma (born 1940)	1963–2004	716	2
Madan Mohan (1924–75)	1950–75	220	2
Naushad Ali (1919–2006)	1940–2005	168	3
Rahul Dev Burman (1939–94)	1961–94	376	3

(*Continued*)

(Continued)

Name	Period Active as a Composer of Hindi Songs	Number of Songs for Lata Mangeshkar	Number of Songs in the Collection
Rajesh Roshan (born 1955)	1974–present	120	1
Ravindra Jain (1944–2015)	1972–2015	41	1
Roshan Lal Nagrath (1917–67)	1948–67	150	4
Sachin Dev Burman (1906–75)*	1944–75	202	2
S. Mohinder (1925–2020)	1948–66	16	1
Sajjad Hussain (1917–95)	1944–77	17	1
Salil Chowdhury (1925–95)*	1952–95	158	2
Shankar (1922–1987) Jaikishan (1929–71)	1949–86	465	6
Shyam Sundar (1906–53)*	1939–53	22	1
Vasant Desai (1912–75)	1942–75	150	1

* The years of birth of SD and Salil Chowdhury are per official records. However, according to RD Burman, son of SD, his father was born in 1901. And as per salilda.com, the website on Salil Chowdhury maintained by Gautam Choudhury, his year of birth was 1922 or 1923.

* The birth year of Shyam Sundar is per scribe Sharad Dutt.

Lyricist

Name	Number of Songs for Lata Mangeshkar	Number of Songs in the Collection
Abhilash (1946–2020)	2	1
Amit Khanna (born 1951)	24	1
Anand Bakshi (1930–2002)	781	3
Behzad Lucknavi (1900–74)	3	1
Hasrat Jaipuri (1922–99)	309	3
Indivar (1924–97)	170	1
Kaif Bhopali (1917–91)	8	1
Kaifi Azmi (1919–2002)	54	3
Khumar Barabankvi (1919–99)	33	1
Majrooh Sultanpuri (1919–2000)	451	6
Meerabai (1498–1547)	38	1
Mir Taqi Mir (1723–1810)	1	1
Mirza Ghalib (1797–1869)	11	1
Naqsh Lyallpuri (1928–2017)	32	1
Narendra Sharma (1913–89)	87	1
Nazim Panipati (1920–98)	10	1
Prem Dhawan (1923–2001)	199	1
Qamar Jalalabadi (1917–2003)	80	1

(Continued)

(Continued)

Name	Number of Songs for Lata Mangeshkar	Number of Songs in the Collection
Raja Mehdi Ali Khan (1915–66)	68	1
Rajendra Krishan (1919–87)	557	2
Ravindra Jain (1944–2015)	31	1
Sahir Ludhianvi (1921–80)	170	4
Satyendra Athaiya (?–2004)	8	1
Shailendra (1923–66)	379	5
Shakeel Badayuni (1916–70)	204	3
Sumita Kumari Sinha (1913–94)	1	1
Tanvir Naqvi (1919–72)	21	1
Udhav Kumar (?)	14	1
Yogesh (1943–2020)	53	1

A young Lata Mangeshkar, artwork by Prachitee Tushar Shetty

1 In the beginning

Lata Mangeshkar first recorded a Hindi film song for the Marathi film *Gajabau* in 1943. The music director was Datta Davjekar (1917–2007), who is reputed to be someone with great foresight. He refused to remain a traditionalist and experimented with electronically generated sounds in the 1970s, and was sought after by musicians like Kersi Lord (1935–2016) and music directors like Rahul Dev Burman.

Davjekar was also the music director of Lata's first song in Hindi cinema, 'Pao lagoo kar jori re', from the 1947 film *Aap ki sewa mein* (whose lyrics were written by Mahipal Chandra Bhandari, credited mononymously as Mahipal, the name he also went by as an actor). Later, Davjekar also assisted Lata when she composed under the nom de plume Anandghan.

However, Lata's rise to prominence in Hindi cinema in the late 1940s was due to composers Master Ghulam Haider, Masterji Khemchand Prakash and Anil Biswas. This part of the book is about the songs Lata chose from their kitty for the album under discussion.

Master Ghulam Haider – the melody queen maker

Song

- 'Dil mera toda' (*Majboor*, 1948)
  - Lyrics: Nazim Panipati

Namaskar. Triggered by the enthusiasm of my listeners, I selected fifty songs on the completion of forty years of my work as a playback singer (as lip-syncing singers are called in India). *Simultaneously, I was constantly mulling over the thought that while the songs are my favourites, would they be the favourites of my listeners as well? Gradually, the verdicts started pouring in. Some via letters, and some directly. People liked my selection, though there were complaints from a few as well. I am happy to mention that you sent repeated requests to roll out a select list of my favourites once more.*

There is a reason behind any song that I choose. Some are because I like the melody, while there are times when the lyrics of some move me. It could be that I love the orchestration of a few, while a song might trigger a memory. A connected one.

Like the first song in my current selection. Dil mera toda. The film was Majboor. The song has a behind the scenes story that suddenly brought me in the limelight. The composer of the song was the famous Master Ghulam Haider of yesteryears. He once called me at Filmistan studio and got me to sing for a producer who opined – 'her voice is too thin.' Masterji was deeply insulted by this abrupt rejection, and said, 'Lata, come with me.' We went to Goregaon station, and while waiting for the train, Masterji, using his tin of cigarettes as the rhythm instrument, sang a tune to me, and asked me to sing it as well. I tried. He immediately said – 'now you must record it.'

When people came to know that Master Ghulam Haider is recording a new voice, word spread like wildfire in the film industry. And I started getting singing assignments from all directions. Something which is still happening by God's grace and your prayers.

This is how the album *LM – Vol 2* starts.[1]

* * *

To recount the full story, let us go back to the mid-1940s, when a team led by Sasadhar Mukerji (1907–90, aka Shashdhar/ Sashadhar/S. Mukerji), Ashok Kumar (1911–2001), et al., had left Bombay Talkies (BT)[2] studio in 1943 to launch Filmistan[3] in Goregaon, Bombay. In those days, while studios had crews on term contracts, freelancing was also accepted. And while it was Filmistan that provided Master Ghulam Haider with a break in Bombay with their first film, *Chal Chal re Naujawan* (1944), it was as a freelancer that he established himself. He already had a successful tenure in Lahore. *Khazanchi* (1941) had made him a star. His *Khandan* (1942) was the breakthrough for Noor Jehan (1926–2000), the most popular female singer of the 1940s in the subcontinent. Hence it was not just humiliation for Haider that his choice of singer was rejected by Mukerji. Lata too might have felt insulted, as despite being a newcomer at that time, her 'thin' tone matched the lead for whom she was tested as the playback. Kamini Kaushal, who was known for her weak and delicate voice.

* * *

Lata's journey with Haider had begun on an interesting note. The makers of *Khazanchi* had organized a music competition where the participants had to sing two songs from the film. From a whopping 114 girls, Lata, then twelve, was the winner. One of the judges was Haider.

Around five years later, in an audition in front of Haider, she bungled up the beat while singing one of his compositions. She later attributed this to nerves. After hearing that Lata had trained under Amanat Khan (1901–48?)[4], Haider's confidence in her abilities was restored. Rejection at Filmistan was followed by BT generously accepting Haider's choice.

What followed is now regarded as a major steppingstone in the history of playback singing in India. But before that, India was declared independent. And the partition happened.

Masterji – Khemchand Prakash
Song

- 'Chanda re ja re ja re' (*Ziddi*, 1948)
  - Prem Dhawan

Partition, predating India's independence in 1947, remains a turning point in the country's social, economic, religious and political history. It came with its woes. In an act of vigorous reshuffling, those who were not killed during the rampant violence and retaliatory riots that were triggered off in 1946 and carried over for years shifted to the country of their choice. Hindus, in the newly formed West Pakistan and East Bengal (later renamed East Pakistan, which then became the independent country of Bangladesh), travelled to India. Many Muslims went to Pakistan and East Bengal. Prominent among them were towering figures like writer Saadat Hasan Manto and singer Noor Jehan.

Ghulam Haider too chose to migrate, leaving India with one 'Masterji' less. This departure of somebody who had just begun shaping the phenomenon called Lata Mangeshkar happened barely a few months after he had composed for her and could have had a detrimental effect on her career. But on the horizon was Khemchand Prakash, another 'Masterji', who, after a five-year long film career in Calcutta which included an assistantship under Timir Baran (1904–87), had shifted to Bombay in 1939 at the request of Chandulal Shah (1898–1975), the owner of Ranjit Studios. Like Haider, he too had an ear for the unconventional and supreme confidence in his choices. Kishore Kumar (1929–87), arguably India's most lauded male playback of all time, was one such. And he had Lata Mangeshkar as his singing partner inside the precinct of BT.

It was around early 1948 when Masterji Khemchand Prakash summoned Lata Mangeshkar and Kishore Kumar to sing a duet for the lead actors in *Ziddi* (1948). Kishore Kumar sang for Dev Anand (1923–2011). It was his first duet.[5] Lata eventually sang for Kamini Kaushal.[6]

That brings us to the second song Lata chose in the album, 'Chanda re ja re ja re'. If 'Dil mera toda' was a motif Lata cherished on account of nostalgia, 'Chanda re ja re ja re' was mostly about musical form and competence. 'Form', because the raag Nat-based phrase 'Piya se sandesha mora kahiyo ja' was later used in songs more than one, including the legendary comic number 'Ek Chatur Naar' (*Padosan*, 1968). The tune became one of the unacknowledged anthems in BT. However, this phrase is not an original, and there have been multiple instances where it has been used before, especially in Bengal by Himanghsu Dutta (1908–44) and Sachin Dev Burman. 'Natun phagune jabe', a 1936 release composed by Dutta and sung by SD, had almost the same mukhra, set in a slightly different beat and tempo. SD and Prakash shared the music room at BT, and this could have been an instance where SD influenced his colleague. Or Prakash might have picked it up during his days in Calcutta.

Lata's admiration for the song was more from a technical point of view. The song was replete with continuous phrases and a plethora of notes, giving the singer precious little time to complete one before jumping to the next. One would run out of breath.

Talking of breath control, another maestro got it right for Lata.

* * *

* A year later, Khemchand Prakash gave Lata 'Aayega aane wala' (*Mahal*, 1949), the song that would change the system of labelling of shellacs in the country. Till then, film songs on shellacs, including those of *Mahal*, did not have the name of the playback artiste but credited the on-screen character instead (not even the actor) who 'sang' it. The success of *Mahal* and the subsequent clamour from the listening public demanding to know the identity of the actual singer compelled HMV to begin crediting playback singers on the label. Prakash did not live to see his huge success.

Anil Biswas – the first star

Songs

- 'Tumhare bulane ko' (*Ladli*, 1949)
    - Lyrics: Behzad Lucknavi

- 'Jhil mil sitaron ke tale' (*Naaz*, 1954)
    - Lyrics: Satyendra Athaiya

Universally known as the 'Bhishma Pitamaha' among Hindi cine music composers, Anil Biswas arrived in Bombay in the mid-1930s from Calcutta, where he had worked as a music assistant in plays, apart from being on the payroll of Hindusthan Musical Products as a voice trainer. It was probably the latter attribute for which Lata Mangeshkar remembered him most. That he trained Lata in the art of unobtrusive breathing between notes is part of music history. Ghulam Haider was her first great guru; he had guided her to use the microphone to get the best sound quality. Examples included taking short 'taans', getting the proper enunciation of the lyrics and singing at a higher volume during the beat at the end of the cycle. Similarly, Biswas was an expert when it came to obliterating the 'hiss' of a sharp breath intake that would otherwise sound discordant. His experience of composing for the stage gave him the additional knowledge of throwing the voice. Lata's voice was feeble. She was also very young. Despite these limitations, Lata sounded clear and sharp from the late 1940s, her voice going from strength to strength in the years to come. One needs to appreciate that music recordings for the cinema in India were in its infancy then. The studio floor often proxied for the recording studio. In the absence of proper insulation, recordings would happen at night to avoid extraneous noise being picked up, with the singer often sharing a single microphone with the orchestra. Biswas also coached her on aspects of fading in and fading out to hit a note, striking the sweet spot on the mike, and maintaining optimal distance from the microphone.

There is also an unsaid, implicit part to Biswas's music: his knowledge of Hindustani classical music. Having a brother-in-law in expert flautist Pannalal Ghosh (1911–60) also helped, though the grapevine has it that Biswas would help Ghosh and not vice versa for compositions for the cinema, a case in point being Phani Majumdar's (1911–94) *Andolan* (1951).

Moving on to Lata's favourites of Biswas selected for the album. Both 'Tumhare bulane ko' from *Ladli* (1949) and 'Jhil mil sitaron ke tale' from *Naaz* (1954) are fast-paced, and one does not find Hindustani classical dominating the proceedings. These are songs where the instruments are important cogs in the wheel. Especially the piano, which fulfils its role as a strike instrument as well by maintaining the tempo.

A piece of trivia about Behzad Lucknavi, the poet who also worked in Hindi cinema. As his name suggests, he was from Lucknow, and folklore has it that he would, in the manner of Majnu (of *Laila Majnu* fame), write the name of Akhtari Bai aka Begum Akhtar (1914–74), the famous singer, on the walls of the city, professing his love for her.

Lata's connection with Khemchand Prakash and Anil Biswas happened during the campaign started by Ghulam Haider. It is said that God sends his angels somewhere, somehow. Lata found the three who laid the cornerstones on which her edifice could stand on its own, during times when she needed it most. The Lata Mangeshkar post the mid-1940s might not have been there if a certain Ghulam Haider had not placed confidence on a kid who was out of work after a certain Master Vinayak (1906–47), Lata's first mentor, had passed away. And two music maestros who trusted Haider's ear. Haider left for Pakistan, Prakash died early, but Biswas continued to compose for Lata till he bid adieu to cinema and moved to Delhi in the mid-1960s.

By the early 1950s, the trailblazers had taken control.

Notes

1 Lata Mangeshkar's speech in Hindi at the beginning of '*My Favourites Volume 2*' translated by the authors.

2 Film studio founded by Himansu Rai (1892–1940) in 1934 in Malad, Bombay.

3 Film studio founded by a section of people who had moved out of Bombay Talkies in 1943.

4 Date as per https://www.parrikar.org/vpl/catalogue/hindustani/amanat-khan/.

5 Kishore Kumar also sang his first published solo in *Ziddi*. He had sung a solo before in *Eight Days* (1946), but it was not published on record.

6 Kamini Kaushal was the heroine in *Ziddi*, as she was in *Shaheed*.

2 The trailblazers

From early 1950 to the mid-1960s, the duo of Shankar and Jaikishan were the commercial kings of Hindi cine music. Their mass-market clout was matched by the quality of music they wrote during their period of dominance. Almost all in the cinema fraternity agreed that their compositions catered to every mood that could be translated into a song situation. Hence, it is no wonder that Lata Mangeshkar, despite having a love-hate relationship with the duo during the mid-to-end 1960s, chose the maximum number of songs, 6, from the 465 songs she sang for them.

Shankar Jaikishan – the allrounders

Songs

- 'Kar gaya re' (*Basant Bahar*, 1956)
  - Lyrics: Shailendra
  - Co-singer: Asha Bhosle
- 'O mora nadaan balma' (*Ujala*, 1959)
  - Lyrics: Hasrat Jaipuri
- 'Aaj kal mein dhal gaya' (*Beti Bete*, 1964)
  - Lyrics: Shailendra

- 'Jeevan ke do raahen pe khade' (*Chhoti Si Mulaqat*, 1967)
    - Lyrics: Shailendra
- 'Aawara aye mere dil' (*Raat aur Din*, 1967)
    - Lyrics: Shailendra
- 'Mera watan Japan' (*Aman*, 1967)
    - Lyrics: Hasrat Jaipuri

The late 1940s in India were an eventful period in the country's history, just as it was for the country's film music. As we discussed in the previous chapter, both were linked: several prominent music directors and singers migrated to the newly formed Pakistan, while one dulcet voiced, fragile lady was beginning to make her mark – Lata Mangeshkar.

We have also mentioned earlier that Lata had already been singing and recording for a few years from the mid-1940s. However, she could have said to have 'arrived' only with producer-director-impresario Raj Kapoor's (1924–88) *Barsaat* in 1949 – a film that, like a proverbial alignment of planets, also saw the debut of lyric writer poets Shailendra and Hasrat Jaipuri, and not the least, composers Shankar and Jaikishan.

It was a combination that almost did not happen. Raj Kapoor (we shall be often using the acronym RK when referring to Raj Kapoor) had signed Ram Ganguly (?–1983) as the music director, who had scored popular tunes for Raj's previous film *Aag* (1948), with Shankar and Jaikishan retaining their roles as music arrangers. Dattaram Wadkar (1929–2007), who was a percussionist playing the dholak for them, recalled the sequence of events to Dr Rao. A solo song by Lata was to be recorded at Famous Studios in Tardeo, central

Bombay, which had two mirror-image recording rooms with a connecting door. RK and all the musicians had assembled in one of these rooms, awaiting the arrival of Lata and the music director. Presently, Lata entered through the connecting door wearing a puzzled expression, saying, 'I went into the other room by mistake, but Ram Ganguly is in *there*, conducting a separate set of musicians. And the tune is the same as the one *I am* supposed to be singing!' Once he confirmed the veracity of this statement, RK, enraged by Ganguly's sheer gall, sacked him, bundled Shankar and Jaikishan (here henceforth referred to as S-J) off to the office of HMV and officially registered them as the music directors of *Barsaat*.[1]

Lata completely eclipses her fellow singers in the *Barsaat* album, and barring one solo by Mohammed Rafi, features on all tracks, including the lesser-heard (and not issued) 'Prem nagar mein basne walo',[2] which started the S-J trend of using raag Shivranjani for a sad song in an RK film. The SJ-Lata combo became as much a necessary fixture in an RK film as the casting of Raj's frequent costar and muse Nargis (1929–81). Raj's *Boot Polish* (1954) and the lesser-known *Ab Dilli Door Nahin* (1957) were rare exceptions.

S-J's catchy tunes, polished orchestration and their uncannily proper choice of singer for a specific song were huge strengths, and in combination with Lata Mangeshkar, their popularity and variety remained unsurpassed for almost two decades. For two films of the 1950s, *Poonam* (1952) and *Aurat* (1953), all songs were Lata solos (nine in each!), and each one of her six songs of *Mayurpankh* (1954) was featured on a different actress. For all the 1950s and most of the 1960s, she was their predominant – often the only – choice (the tiffs came later, from the mid-1960s [*Suraj* (1966)] onwards). As a corollary to this partnership, all the major actresses of the era benefited, their visible on-screen beauty augmented and their share value risen when they lip-synced to Lata's arresting voice.

Lata covered the gamut of emotions and sub-genres in S-J's compositions: she sang devotional *bhajans*, lullabies, romantic solos and duets, cabaret and club songs, songs of pathos and songs tuned in the classical *raags* of India. No wonder Lata had the greatest respect for S-J as composers. She would use the term 'peerless' for the duo, with a preference for Jaikishan's tunes as compared to his senior member Shankar. She also found Jai particularly good-looking.[3,4]

On the aspect of musical versatility, veterans differ. Singer Manna Dey (1919–2013) has gone on record terming Shankar as a genius who considered music his life and the studio his home.[5] Actor Shammi Kapoor (1931–2011) – who had trained in Hindustani classical for a short time – in an interview with scribe and author Balaji Vittal, had mentioned the following: 'Jai was good. But his tunes were simple, easy to hum. Shankar had more depth. His knowledge of Indian classical music was more'.[6] And when any discussion drifts around Indian classical music, few can deny that S-J's favourite among the raags in Hindustani classical was Bhairavi. Shankar called it a 'sada suhagan' ('ever married') raag, and some of the more outstanding Bhairavis of Hindi film music are theirs, right from the title song of *Barsaat*, 'Suno chhotisi gudiya ki lambi kahani' from *Seema* (1955) (with an arresting sarod intro by maestro Ali Akbar Khan (1922–2009)), 'Kabhi to aa' (*Patrani*, 1956) and dozens of others up until the 1975 film *Sanyasi* in which all songs were in that raag.

One criticism has been that S-J consistently tuned her songs to a needlessly high pitch, a point mentioned to Dr Rao by Lata's sister Asha Bhosle, who felt the same of their compositions for her too (especially her duets with Mohammed Rafi (1924–80)).[7] It is likely that S-J felt that no other female voices could scale those peaks, which might also explain why the maximum number of Lata's female duets, ninety-two in all, are with Asha.

Such an intimate association over decades as Lata's was with S-J would inevitably spring cracks. Multiple causes have been implicated and theories formulated: arguments over perceived vulgarities in lyrics; Shankar's liaison with and promotion of another singer named Sharda in the mid-1960s; Lata insisting on royalty payments even from RK, who had always viewed her as a regular RK staffer on payroll; a certain cooling off between Shankar and Jaikishan themselves, all culminating in Jaikishan's death in 1971.

Consequently, no S-J song figured in either Lata's silver jubilee celebrations held in 1967 or in her lavish three-day concert at London's Royal Albert Hall in 1974. She pointedly refused to sing for RK's magnum opus *Mera Naam Joker* (1970) if Shankar was the composer; Raj stood by Shankar, but following that film's failure, abandoned him and crossed the floor to sign on Laxmikant and Pyarelal (and Lata) for his next venture, *Bobby* (1973). Thus ended the glorious RK/S-J association, but such are the cat's cradle associations of showbiz that subsequently Lata made up with Shankar and continued to sing under his baton for many more years to come. However, no song of S-J for RK featured in our album under discussion. Point to note: the number of S-J compositions she earmarked for inclusion was six – the highest among all composers included in the album.

* * *

The first of the six is 'Kar gaya re', a song that stands out from the rest of Lata's favourites in that it is one of only two female duets in the compilation. Her co-singer is her equally preeminent sister Asha Bhosle, and most of their duets together have been under the baton of Shankar Jaikishan.

In summary, Shailendra's lyrics have both leading ladies [Kumkum (1934–2020) and Nimmi (1932–2020), one dancing playfully and the other morosely strumming a *tanpura*] chiding the hero for callously stealing their hearts.

One may ponder why Lata chose this song over another Lata-Asha duet from *Sharada* (1957), 'O chand jahan woh jaaye', from the same era. That one too has intricate embellishments (*murkis* and *harkats*) but was executed individually there. In contrast, 'Kar gaya re', couched in raag Bageshri/Abhogi, following a sitar introduction, has an *alaap* sung by both sisters with such congruent perfection that it takes a moment to realize there are two voices, not one.

Kumkum seemed to be on Lata's mind when selecting numbers for the album. 'O mora nadaan baalma', the second song, has more dancing by her. Written by Hasrat Jaipuri for *Ujala* (1959), it is, once again, a theme of unrequited love, but not because the object of the woman's affection was heartless but simply because he was too naïve to feel the vibes.

S-J reprised the title track of another film from a few years earlier, *Mayurpankh*, for the tune. What stands out as much as Lata's rendition is the magnificent *dholak* accompaniment in

6/8 rhythm (*khemta*) by Abdul Karim, the younger brother of music director Ghulam Mohammed. So impressed were then musicians Laxmikant and Pyarelal that when an opportunity arose in the 1960s to score 'Mera naam hai Chameli', a dance number for Kumkum, they too sought out Abdul Karim – partly as a tribute, and partly as light-hearted competition to this S-J song. The song from *Raja aur Runk* (1968), a film based on Mark Twain's *The Prince and the Pauper*, remains a chartbuster.

* * *

A recurrent feature of Hindi film music has been the tandem song, where two versions of a song appear in a film: one slow and one fast, or one sad and one happy or one male and one female. 'Aal kal mein dhal gaya' from *Beti Bete* (1964) belongs to this last category, and it is our authors' opinion that Lata's version outclasses that of her male counterpart. Shailendra's lyrics for this lullaby (as sung on-screen by pre-teen Farida to her younger siblings) are heartfelt enough, but Lata's soulful rendition and S-J's strings' harmony deepening the dramatic impact have made this a song for the ages. Point to note: 1964 had a few blockbusters by S-J, films that included *Sangam*, *Ayee Milan ki bela* and *Rajkumar*. Songs from these films were all over the place. Bypassing the popular choices, Lata selected this quieter, uncelebrated one.

This brings us to another tandem from the team. 'Aawara aye mere dil', and this time both renditions, one happy and one sad, are by Lata for the film *Raat Aur Din* (1967). Lata chooses the fast version for her compilation. Famed actor Nargis, who had retired after *Mother India* made a comeback here, playing a woman who is psychologically disturbed following her mother's premature death. Her behaviour is normal by day, but she becomes a partying alcoholic by night. Unusually, it is the slow version that appears in the film first, with the fast one coming in a later flashback that tries to explain the exact reason for her condition.

Mentally afflicted Nargis roams the deserted streets at night and sings the slow version that is full of languid strings, while the vivacious Laxmi Chhaya (1948–2004) does the fast two-step version, drum rolls, accordion and all. This song also has an all-women chorus, used in the interludes and as the coda.

Lata probably had a soft corner for the film. The earlier volume of *My Favourites* had 'Dil ki girah khol do', another song from *Raat aur Din*. This was her last 1960s film for S-J, where she had six songs. The title song, again a tandem version – the male version was sung by Mukesh (1923–76) – continues to remain a huge hit. It needed no promotion.

* * *

Shailendra, as mentioned earlier, was one of two regular lyricists for S-J. Many, including Lata, have gone on record to mentionthat Shailendra was their favourite lyricist. So, it comes as no surprise to find yet another song penned by him among her favourites, composed by S-J.

This was for a film produced by Uttam Kumar (1926–80), Bengal's greatest star. Based on *Agni Pariksha* (1954), an early hit in his career, this was to be his launching pad in Bombay after a few false starts, one of which was refusing the role later played by Rajendra Kumar (1927–99) in RK's *Sangam*. The film, named *Chhoti Si Mulaqat*, was a miserable failure. While there are multiple conspiracy theories in circulation, ranging from budget overshoots manoeuvred by a star and filmmaker to Uttam being forced to take a rookie director, thankfully no fancy stories have sprung up about the music. It was vintage S-J, with the Lata solo 'Jeevan ke do raahen pe khade' being the jewel in the crown.

On screen is the beautiful Vyjayantimala, the lithe dancer within her completely restrained, as she stands virtually motionless and sings of indecision while at the crossroads of life. The poet speaks about the myriad conflicts that love brings about – between reality and dreams, pain and pleasure, and sleep and wakefulness. A composition mixing raags Tilak Kaamod and Khamaj,[8] the pitching in D sharp scale helps in drawing attention to the angst. One is tempted to find likenesses with the compositions of Madan Mohan, whose tunes for Lata are noted for their melancholy. Moreso, due to S-J's musical accompaniment, which consists of a small ensemble of sitar, tabla, saxophone and strings. Uttam, with his experience of working in Bengali films where song shoots would often be with real musicians,[9] ensured that the musicians' finger movements were coordinated with what was being played. The song brings to mind another S-J/Lata number of a few years later, also set in a recording studio, with a similar melodic structure: 'Devta maana aur pooja teri tasveer ko' (*Albela*, 1971).[10] The stanza (antara) might have acted as an inspiration for the young pair Kalyanji (1928–2000) and Anandji (Born 1933) – in their use of mid-range notes. The song could also have been the template for S-J themselves while composing the title song of *Nadaan* (1971) for Mukesh.

Unfortunately, even a song of this stature could not prevent *Chhoti Si Mulaqat* from sinking, despite the original Bengali language version having been a crowd favourite.

* * *

Talking of languages, several songs of S-J carried an opening line in a foreign language, that of the country in which the film was set – 'Rasa sayang re' (Malay for 'loving feeling') in *Singapore* (1960), 'Ich Liebe dich' ('I love you' in German) in *Sangam* and the well-known 'Sayonara' ('Goodbye' in Japanese) from *Love in Tokyo* (1966).

It was a pleasant surprise to find Lata choosing 'Mera watan Japan' from *Aman* (1967) ('Peace'), also shot in Japan and like 'Sayonara', composed by S-J in a typical Japanese template (knowledgeable Indian listeners will identify the structure as raag Bhoopali) in addition to using traditional Japanese instruments such as koto and taiko, and the xylophone. While it is certainly not expected of a leading lady to announce her nationality and sing paeans in praise of her country when she is romancing the hero, the audience in the 1960s were a forgiving lot. They assumed stupidity was acceptable if the music was pleasing to the ear. And the heroine beautiful. The song and Saira Banu, the heroine, both fulfilled these requirements. The occasional questions by the cerebral lot did not deter filmmakers from sticking to set patterns. Saira Banu's skin and complexion were comparable to the best of Japanese women. Her features were to die for; she could have been a beauty pageant winner in any country in the world. The song she lip-synched was not only tuneful, but it was also eminently hummable. Composers, lyricists and singers in the Hindi film industry rose much above the mundane films in which they were employed.

In this case, the first words are 'Aisuru, aisuru' ('Love, love'), and Lata gives the opening 'Ai' syllable an arresting accentuation that nails the Japanese effect. To rhyme with 'Mera watan Japan' (my country is Japan), lyricist Hasrat Jaipuri incorporates its synonymous Japanese equivalent ('furusato Japan').

To top it, Saira Banu's character's Indo-Japanese charms and excellent aerial photography, from Mount Fuji to the nightlife of Tokyo, make it a full house of audio-visual pleasure.

Some eighteen years before an Indian stunner was singing *Watashi no kuni wa Nihondesu*, Madhubala (1933–69), who had the tagline 'the Venus of the Indian screen', looked no less gorgeous dancing to 'Taqdeer jaga kar aayi hoon' in a studio masquerading as a garden in *Dillagi* (1949). A. R. Kardar (1904–89), the director of the film, would have the name of the music director of *Dillagi* (1949) in *Dastan* (1950), his next film, as part of the trailer – *Challish karore mein ek hi Naushad* [Naushad, the only one in forty crores (forty crores was the estimated population of India at that time)].[11] More about him and the likes in the next chapter 'The Classicists'.

Notes

1 Interview with Dattaram by Dr Chandrashekar Rao.

2 https://www.youtube.com/watch?v=Noe2aNZdM3g.

3 Yatindra Mishra, *Lata Sur Gatha* (New Delhi: Vani Prakashan, 2016), Pages 285–6.

4 Nasreen Munni Kabir, *Lata in Her Own Voice* (London: Hyphen Films, for Channel Four, 1990).

5 Manna Dey, *Jeeboner Jalsaghare* (Kolkata: Ananda, 2005), Pages 139–40.

6 Interview with Shammi Kapoor by Balaji Vittal in 2008.

7 Interview with Asha Bhosle by Dr Chandrashekhar Rao.

8 Raag names as per email discussion with musicologist K. L. Pandey on 3 November 2023.

9 Uttam produced *Deya Neya* (1963) where song recordings were shown having actual musicians.

10 https://youtu.be/7gaJLN3Gug0?si=T31R9JHvludwqdES.

11 Pankaj Rag, *Dhunon ki Yatra* (New Delhi: Rajkamal Prakashan, 2006), Page 129.

3 The classicists

By definition, a classicist is someone who follows the principles of classicism in their chosen area of work. Naushad, SD, Roshan and Jaidev, composers who were very dear to Lata, embodied the definition very strongly, though Burman would, at a later stage, modify his style to suit changing tastes. The following section covers the songs Lata chose from their compositions.

Naushad – the 'Lucknavi' master

Songs

- 'Taqdeer jaga kar aayi hoon' (*Dulari*, 1949)
  - Lyrics: Shakeel Badayuni
- 'Do sitaron ka zameen' (*Kohinoor*, 1960)
  - Lyrics: Shakeel Badayuni
  - Co-singer: Md. Rafi
- 'Tere pyaar mein dildaar' (*Mere Mehboob*, 1963)
  - Lyrics: Shakeel Badayuni

Naushad's is a name that automatically inspires reverence not merely because he was venerable, age-wise, but because his strengths were manifold: he was trained in Hindustani classical music and was skilled at weaving raga-based melodies; he played the piano and could read and write scores in western music; as a boy, he was already part of an orchestra that played live music to go with silent films in a pre-talkie-era Lucknow, an experience that instilled in him a firm grasp on timing a composed piece to serve as a film's background score.

When Lata Mangeshkar was coming into her own in the late 1940s while still in her teens, it was only natural that most composers who worked with her would be her senior. Naushad was no exception and was a whole decade older, and their first film together was Mehboob Khan's (1907–64) *Andaz* in 1949. But while she outgrew (or outlived) many of her other mentors, her collaboration with Naushad lasted through films released over the next forty-five years, the last being the Shah Rukh Khan starrer *Guddu* in 1995 – which must be some kind of record (fittingly, the lyricist in both *Andaz* and *Guddu* was Majrooh Sultanpuri). Yet these films did not number in the hundreds, like the output of Shankar Jaikishan or Laxmikant Pyarelal; in his entire career, Naushad scored music for only sixty-five films. This was not for dearth of offers – he was picky and worked hard on giving every song a meticulous polish. The finished product was invariably a connoisseur's delight; one could scarcely imagine a specific lyric being couched in any other tune or raga.

Lata Mangeshkar fainting during a song recording of Naushad is an oft-told anecdote, such was the complexity of his tune as was her determination to get it right (a recurring *murki* was the challenge, though Lata's version pinned it down to the recording studio's unbearable heat). For whatever it is, Naushad's image was built and preserved well. Extremely hard-working and genuinely good at his craft, he had leadership qualities that extended to managing the media as well. Inasmuch, in the 1960s, he had written to Filmfare, questioning why the film critics never spoke about the music in their film reviews. The response he received was not exactly complimentary; nevertheless, he did have a symbiotic relationship with the media, just as he had with his favourite singers, Lata Mangeshkar and Md. Rafi.

And, of course, with lyricist Shakeel Badayuni. Post *Andaz*, Naushad worked mostly with him for eighteen years at a stretch, till illness forced Shakeel to stop writing altogether in 1968. Hence, it is no surprise that all three Naushad songs of Lata's choosing are written by his frequent (and perhaps favourite) collaborator, Shakeel Badayuni.

Lata Mangeshkar's voice was one of the reasons behind the sudden rise in popularity of actress Madhubala. 'Taqdeer jaga kar ayi hoon', which finds a young Madhubala singing about the awakenings of love, is a simple ditty, with bare minimum orchestration, befitting her innocent and naive character. This was in 1949, the first year of the Lata-Naushad collaboration. While the picturization might seem primitive today, the filming was ahead of its time, being shot in just two continuous takes with the camera on a trolley.

Like the previous song in the selection, on screen, 'Do sitaron ka zameen' also has the set masquerading as the outdoors, this time a mountain. Naushad, particular about the locale, used raag Pahadi ('mountainous') and supplemented the main song with a delicate prelude using string instruments. His use of 'Pahadi' here was different from the Pahadi dhun he used for Lata's 'Tod diya dil mera' (*Andaz*) or 'Marna teri gali mein' (*Shabab*, 1954). It has a more rapturous quality, where melancholy does not interfere. Md. Rafi remains the singer with whom Lata has sung the most duets, 459, and this song is one of the many where their voices not only blend but also stand out individually like colours in an impressionist painting, where Rafi's suppleness and feather-light touch are complemented by Lata's flawless pitching. The three-second-long choral backup, paced in Dadra (3/4 rhythm) and used in both the antaras, augments the feeling of longing that has remained unspoken till then.

Unspoken sentiments often can make you get into a vortex, and in Hindi cinema, filmmakers create special song situations for these moments. As in the case with 'Tere pyar mein dildaar', where Sadhana, the heroine, confides her treasured secret to her cousin, played by Ameeta. The character for whom the song is composed is a conservative Muslim, and the song must be sung indoors. Understandably, the lyrics are in chaste Urdu, in keeping with the film's Aligarh-Lucknow milieu.

Naushad's choice of Bihag is an excellent fit, as the raag sounds best if sung in the mid-octave. And secrets are surely not to be shouted about.

From one secret confession by a purist, we move to a nightcap by another.

Sachin Dev Burman – the folkman from Bengal

Songs

- 'Chand phir nikla' (*Paying Guest*, 1957)
    - Lyrics: Majrooh Sultanpuri

- 'Soch ke ye gagan jhoomen' (*Jyoti*, 1969)
    - Lyrics: Anand Bakshi
    - Co-singer: Manna Dey

SD (aka Dada Burman/Dada), a singer of great repute, especially of Bengali folk and semiclassical songs, came to Bombay from Calcutta in October 1944 at the invitation of Sasadhar Mukerji and Ashok Kumar. They had just stepped out of BT and founded Filmistan. In Bombay, a series of failures had made SD circumspect of the future, and by 1949, he had decided to go back to the more artistic and complacent Calcutta. A newly built house at the southern end of the city awaited him.

Two things happened. Brothers Chetan (1921–97) and Dev Anand floated Navketan, a film production company and offered SD to compose for them. And Ashok Kumar, who had bought the rights to BT in 1948, invited SD to compose for the bilingual *Mashal* (1950) (Hindi)/*Samar* (1950) (Bengali).

It was during the sittings of *Mashal* that SD met Lata. Mutual admiration happened instantaneously. Post-*Barsaat* and *Mahal*, Lata was a star, inasmuch, she was one of the few to move in a car which she had purchased in 1948 or 1949. Recordings in those days happened mostly after sunset, when the sound of the ambient traffic would not seep into the studios. A particular song recording went late into the night, and SD and his secretary, Sachin Ganguly, were given a lift by Lata. The atmosphere in the studio was like family, and the sittings and the subsequent success of *Mashal* meant that the human bond, something SD thought would be elusive in a place like Bombay, was suddenly formed. He, who would have a regular quota of basic (non-film) songs in Calcutta, did not find the need or the time to record a single Bengali song in the next five years.

He had found the voice of his choice too.

Very soon, Lata was singing most of his compositions. For example, *Buzdil* (1951), despite having a theme around the 'buzdil (coward)', Kishore Sahu, the male lead, had Lata sing five of the six songs, including the iconic 'Jhan jhan jhan jhan payal baaje', one that SD himself had sung before. It was based on a thumri by Ustad Faiyaz Khan (1886–1950). SD and Faiyaz Khan both recorded for Hindusthan Musical Products, and one assumes that it was on the ground floor at Akrur Dutta Lane, Calcutta,[1] that SD might have sought permission to record Khan Saheb's thumri.

Dev Anand, who would have nobody but SD for his productions, was fascinated by SD's singing and would mention that none could fully reproduce the notes he hit, except for Lata. Hence, it is not without reason that Lata would choose at least one SD favourite from a Dev Anand film. *Volume 1* had 'Phaili hui hai sapno ki baahen' from *House Number 44* (1955), a lesser-known song that gained popularity via the audio cassettes industry, with an HMV compilation of songs from Navketan in 1985 starting it all. For *Volume 2*, Lata chose a more conventional and famous song, 'Chand phir nikla', that was shot in a studio impersonating a full moon night from a terrace in Lucknow.

One assumes that the song was composed as an alternative to the discarded 'Rut phire par din hamare' (sung by Geeta Dutt (1930–72)) from *Pyaasa* (1957). One cannot be sure though. However, the songs have similar phrases, as does the Shankar Jaikishan composition 'Rasik Balma' (*Chori Chori*, 1956).

A curious case of three songs having similar phrasing being composed at the same time.

Burying suspicions like who influenced whom, one can go ahead and admire the song simply from the point of view of its excellence. Suddha Kalyan, the raag on which this song is based, was among Lata's favourite raags, and she had also gone on record mentioning that listening to Bade Ghulam Ali Khan (1902–68) singing Kalyan at music conferences would leave her mesmerized. One guesses that this could have been after Khan Saheb invited her on stage in 1952 at a concert in Calcutta.[2]

* * *

Dulal Guha's (1929–2001) *Jyoti* (1969) was launched in 1968 with Meena Kumari (1933–72) and Dharmendra, both big stars then. SD, who was yet to start work on *Aradhana* (1969), a film that would catapult his career to great heights, was free and accepted *Jyoti* at the insistence of producer Alexander Devidas. Devidas was a member of the Football Association in Bombay and knew SD well, as both were regulars at football matches happening at the Cooperage Stadium.[3] By the time work commenced, the leads had been replaced by Sanjeev Kumar and Libi Rana (aka Nivedita), actors from Guha's 1969 film *Dharti Kahe Pukar Ke*, which was on the floor.[4]

Putul Guha, Dulal Guha's son, mentions,[5]

> One day, at 5 AM in the morning, the phone in our hall rang. I was the one who answered the call. On the other side was a sweet but stentorian voice – *Dulal aache? Ami Sachin Dev Burman bolchi* (Is Dulal there? I am Sachin Dev Burman). I woke up my father who hurriedly set out for SD's house on Linking

Road. He returned after a few hours, with the news that SD had created a cracker of a tune.

The song was 'Soch ke ye gagan jhoomen', Lata's second and final choice from SD's stable.

Unfortunately, in the absence of saleable stars, the film did badly. The music, including this duet, had no takers. Records' sales often depended on the success of the film. In thIs case, as *Jyoti* had hardly reached the intended audience, the associated blaze of publicity was missed.

One infers that this selection in *Volume 2* helped the song enter its second life. It became a huge favourite on television, with people often debating the relative beauty of the melody and the lead actress, who was one of the most angelic faces ever to grace Indian cinema.

The composition was inspired by the Bengali song 'Chilo chaand megher paare', written by Ajoy Bhattacharya (1906–43) and composed by Himanghsu Dutta. Incidentally, these two, along with SD, were labelled the 'Comilla triumvirate of melody'.[6] Bhattacharya and Dutta, regular collaborators of SD in Bengali music, had both passed away in the early 1940s.

The musical arrangement was by RD, SD's son, and one might notice the use of a filler music from RD's composition 'Tumne mujhe dekha' (*Teesri Manzil*, 1966) for the first interlude. RD was surely instrumental in the more popular song from *Jyoti*, the Limelight theme (1952)-based lullaby 'Sun munne mere', the stanza of which he would remodel for 'Kali palak teri gori' in 1972 for the film *Do Chor*. The unavailability of good prints of the film drove the song to near oblivion. Lata did not include the lullaby in any of her compilations. Oversight? Most probably.

One can't thank her enough, though, for remembering 'Soch ke yeh'. Even today, Lata – Manna Dey duets are broadly classified as Shankar Jaikishan-RK songs and the rest. However, when it comes to the best, 'Soch ke yeh' has few competitors. The song too is like a competition where both the singers coexist happily while battling out for supremacy, where Lata's pitch-perfect straight notes are matched by Manna's flawless throws with sudden inflexions, his open-throated singing finding a perfect foil in Lata's measured intonation. A bit of Ustad Aman Ali Khan of Bhendibazaar Gharana (1888–1953) in both; a rare instance where the playback singers had the same guru – at least for some time. The full-throated and smooth, jerk-less pitching, especially at high notes, coupled with flawless pronunciation, was representative of their schooling under someone renowned for these.

Roshan – ode to Hindustani classical

Songs

- 'Bade armaano se' (Malhar, 1951)
  - Lyrics: Indivar
  - Co-singer: Mukesh
- 'Mujhe mil gaya bahana' (Barsaat ki Raat, 1960)
  - Lyrics: Sahir Ludhianvi
- 'Jurm-e Ulfat pe' (Taj Mahal, 1963)
  - Lyrics: Sahir Ludhianvi

- 'Sakhi re mera man' (Chitralekha, 1964)
    - Lyrics: Sahir Ludhianvi

'Roshan' was the shortened first name of Roshanlal Nagrath. After his monumental success in the film industry, Roshan become the family name of his music director son Rajesh, actor son Rakesh and actor grandson Hritik. Roshan was born in Gujranwala, in what is today Pakistan's Punjab, and by the time he moved to India, he was steeped in Urdu literature and poetry, while learning classical music in a traditional manner from the likes of Ustad Allaudin Khan and at Marris College, Lucknow (on All India Radio, Roshan was an exponent of the Dilruba, a bowed musical instrument with a sitar-like neck). He also had a good knowledge of the harmonium and the sarangi, among other instruments. These proved to be formidable assets in creating a niche for himself in composing for films, in a sub-genre of his own making that evoked a strongly Urdu-flavoured era of palaces, nawabs, courtesans, ghazals, mujras and (his forte) qawwalis. This was only augmented by frequent collaborations with masterly poets such as Sahir Ludhianvi and polished actors such as Ashok Kumar, Meena Kumari and Pradeep Kumar (1925–2001) playing appropriately regal characters of Indian history (they worked together as a trio in three films scored by Roshan in addition to several others individually).

Lata and Roshan shared a warm relationship, and she had also zeroed in on him when selecting the music director for her shelved film *Bhairavi.*[7] His death, which happened in a split-second while raising a toast to his friend Hari Wallah on the success of his film *Laat Saheb* (1967), almost shocked the industry into temporary silence. It was with welled-up eyes that Lata could record her last song for Roshan, 'Mehlon ka raja mila' (*Anokhi Raat*, 1968), under the supervision of Mrs Ira Roshan.

Lata's last song for Roshan did not make it to *My Favourites*. Instead, 'Bade armaano se', a duet with Mukesh from Mukesh's own production, *Malhar* (1951), did. The only one of the four Roshan songs chosen by Lata Mangeshkar *not* to be penned by Sahir but by Indivar (writing under his original name Shyamalal). Roshan and Mukesh were very close too; and perhaps Lata had this bonding in mind while making the list. Also, the story goes that during this film, Lata, Nargis and Shammi (1929–2018), the leading lady of *Malhar*, become friends. Two songs in the selection were featured on Nargis, who had passed away in 1981. Maybe Lata also wanted to dedicate a song to Shammi, who was still there.

The next three songs are from the pinnacle of Roshan's career. *Barsaat ki Raat* (1960), *Taj Mahal* (1963) and *Chitralekha* (1964) have music that highlights the best of Roshan and of Hindi film music of a particular genre. Let us consider the song from *BKR*. Loosely based on raag Gara, one might be tempted to think that 'Mujhe mil gaya bahana teri deed ka' could be an inspired version of D. V. Paluskar's famous bhajan, 'Raghupati Raghav Raja Ram'. However, Roshan gives the tune a folkish twist, and the instrumentation ensures that it sounds like one. It is a song accentuating the blithe spirit of someone (actress Shyama (1935–2017)) who is in love with hero. Nothing sombre about it.

Taj Mahal embodied a combination of all the composer's strengths, and 'Jurm-e ulfat pe' is a fine example of that amalgam that sets to tune Sahir's beautiful ghazal that expounds the vagaries of love. The film's score justly fetched

Roshan a Filmfare award (India's Oscar equivalent) for Best Music, albeit his only one. By any yardstick, it is a classy choice by Lata for this album, her mellifluous rendition and flawless Urdu diction perfectly complement Roshan's subtle and understated melody couched in raag Gaud Malhar.

Not to miss the opportunity of using a raag whenever possible, the last song of Roshan that Lata selected is in a mix of two raags. Pahadi and Manjh Khamaj. Not sure if 'Sakhi re mera man' was a choice by default. Given an opportunity, we assume that Lata might have picked any of her three songs – the other two being 'Arre jane na dungi' and 'Sansaar se bhage phirte ho' from the film. All of them remain well appreciated by connoisseurs and music lovers of Gen X and before. This was the slightly lesser-known one and needed some marketing effort.

A marketing effort of a different kind happened with Jaidev for his first song with Lata. . . .

Jaidev – the fakir

Songs

- 'Ab tera intezaar kaun kare' (*Joru ka bhai*, 1955)
  - Lyrics: Sahir Ludhianvi
- 'Ek Mithi se Chubhan' (*Reshma aur Shera*, 1971)
  - Lyrics: Udhav Kumar

'Subah ka interzaar kaun kare / Ab tera intezaar kaun kare' from *Joru ka Bhai* is a tandem song where the lyrics are different while the tune is the same. The male version, sung by Talat Mahmood (1924–98), is featured on Balraj Sahni (1913–73), and the female version on his sister in the film, Sheila Ramani (1932–2015).[8] Incidentally, Lata would not have sung this altogether had Sahir Ludhianvi persisted in his unreasonable obstinacy. The temperamental poet and lyricist Sahir was not in talking, terms with Lata for some time during 1954–55. In *Joru ka bhai*, he put in a clause – no Lata. This resulted in Sahir getting replaced, and he returned only after he had made up with her. By then, Vishwamitra Adil (1919–2002) had written seven songs and Narendra Sharma one. The tandem, initially intended to be the first song, was recorded last.[9]

Joru ka Bhai failed. Chetan Anand's attempt to create a lead of his youngest brother Vijay Anand (1934–2004) went nowhere.[10]

This was also Jaidev's first film as an independent composer. While it did not bolster his commercial standing, it made the tandem a fondly remembered one by people who heard it then. And Lata did a great job by putting it on the radar of listeners of Gen X and Y. Sung in a manner most delicate, it has a few soothing passages on the string section and the electronic organ that might remind you of the famous Kishore Kumar solo 'Koi humdum na raha' from *Jhumroo* (1961).

* * *

Reshma aur Shera, on the contrary, was considered by Jaidev to be his best film. Started by documentary filmmaker S. Sukhdev (1933–79), it was completed by the producer and leading man Sunil Dutt (1929–2005). It gave Jaidev his first National award. 'Ek mithi si chubhan', Lata's chosen one in *Vol. 2* was already on a resurrection mode around 1988, as HMV had featured this song in their 12" record collection *Yaadon Ki Manzil* (1986), published to commemorate fifty years of playback singing in India.

The National award did not help. The film was a commercial failure, and Jaidev was, once again, out of work. He attributes his constant struggle to one of the reasons for his unwillingness to marry. Not only that. Jaidev stayed as a paying guest at Lily Court, opposite to the Ritz Hotel near Churchgate station, Bombay. After he died in 1987, his body was taken directly to the crematorium, as he had no family. Per Chhaya Ganguli, who was his student, he was a fakir, destined to spread happiness through music in our lives.[11]

While we are not privy to Lata commenting on Jaidev's stoical lifestyle, she held him in high esteem, especially due to his mastery in compositions based on Hindustani classical music. Her selection of two songs from a total of only thirty-seven spoke about her admiration. As it did in *Volume 1*, where she had chosen two songs as well.

Notes

1. Hindusthan Musical Products was housed at 6/1, Akrur Dutta Lane, Calcutta. The musicians often assembled on the ground floor for evening snacks and to exchange pleasantries.
2. https://www.indiatoday.in/movies/celebrities/story/when-bade-ghulam-ali-khan-said-lata-mangeshkar-was-god-s-gift-1909471-2022-02-06.

3 Soccer matches in Bombay used to happen at Cooperage Stadium.

4 https://www.cinemaazi.com/feature/dulal-guha-his-life-and-times.

5 Interview with Putul Guha in December 2019.

6 SD hailed from Comilla in present-day Bangladesh.

7 Raju Bharatan, *Lata Mangeshkar: A Biography* (New Delhi: UBS Publishers, 1995).

8 As per information from veteran film aficionado Arunkumar Deshmukh.

9 Yasir Abassi, *Yeh Un Dinon Ki Baaṭ Hai* (New Delhi: Bloomsbury, 2018).

10 Interview with Ketan Anand, son of Chetan Anand, on 27 February 2024.

11 Interview with Chhaya Ganguli on 21 February 2024.

4 The conventional

There is a subtle difference between the classicist and the conventional, in the sense that the classicist could deviate and try to adopt to styles different from their own while not circumventing the guidelines prescribed by the genre of music they followed. The conventional, however, would deviate a little. While one would anticipate something new in the work of, say, Naushad or Burman, composers Husnlal Bhagatram, Shyam Sundar and Vasant Desai would prefer to follow a regimental rule that became the hallmark of their music. Lata's work for them was much less compared to the Shankar Jaikishans and the Burmans, and that explains the lesser number of songs she included in the album.

Husnlal Bhagatram – The sound of Punjab

Song

- 'Chale jana nahin' (*Bari Bahen*, 1949)
  - Lyrics: Rajendra Krishan

They were big in the 1940s. The first musical pair in Hindi cinema. Today, few people remember them. Success in the glamour industry is largely transient. That is the unfortunate story of composers Husnlal and Bhagatram, brothers in real life. Hailing from Punjab with expertise over multiple instruments, their music was original and they did have a fair share of the cine music market in the 1940s. The downslide of Husnlal Bhagatram came when faced with a younger lot who changed the way music was created in Bombay cinema. Husnlal Bhagatram had peaked during the time when Shankar Jaikishan debuted and almost steamrolled over any composer following the style of 'heavy orchestration'. The Punjabi school, something that dominated the 1940s and the music of Husnlal Bhagatram, found a more competent student in O. P. Nayyar (1926–2007). Within a noticeably short time, Shankar Jaikishan became SJ, or S-J. Nayyar became O P, or Opee. Husnlal Bhagatram remained, well, Husnlal Bhagatram, and were gradually relegated to the role of instrumentalists in the orchestra.

Luck too played spoilsport.

The duo did not get the best of films. Or banners. Barring a few, the films they signed were inconsequential. And it is courtesy of the songs of one such insignificant film that Lata Mangeshkar, who was close to the duo at a point in time, has remembered them. *Bari Behen* (1949). And the key point remains that Lata's most famous songs for the duo are from a film owned by Suraiya (1929–2004), who was the lead actor and singer. 'Chale jana nahin nain milake' was featured on the second heroine, Geeta Bali (1930–65), singing to the philanderer, Pran, who would ultimately land her in a lot of trouble. Lata had two more songs in the film, 'Chup chup khade ho zaroor koi baat hai' – a frolicsome and trendy duet with Premlata – which is popular even today, and 'Jo dil mein khushi bankar aaye', which nobody remembers.

In hindsight, *Bari Behen* was not as bad a film as it looks today. It had an unwanted pregnancy as the subject, something very bold for its time. But any nostalgia related to the film is because of the music. When Lata played second fiddle to Suraiya. And she could still leave her imprint on the songs. So, it is up to you whether you are enamoured by Suraiya's weepy 'Woh pass rahen ya door rahen' or Lata's blithe spirit in the raag Asavari-based 'Chale jana nahin'.

Or is your favourite of the 1940s 'Sajan ki galiyan chhod chale'?

Shyam Sundar – pathos of Punjab

Song

- 'Sajan ki galiyan chhod chale' (*Bazar*, 1949)
  - Lyrics: Qamar Jalalabadi

The India-Pakistan feud, which started at the time of the partition in 1947, continued for decades. As a result, artistes from either country would be reluctant to visit the other, leading to a complete cultural freeze. Incidents such as Nusrat Fateh Ali Khan being flown to Bombay by RK for his son Rishi Kapoor's wedding in 1980 were exceptions. However, acts like these became precedents, and the 1980s saw many Pakistani artistes visiting India. One of them was Noor Jehan in 1982, who came to India after thirty-five years at the invitation of the then prime minister, Mrs. Indira Gandhi.

Noor Jehan and Lata were the best of friends during the brief period they had worked together in the 1940s. Lata, officially three years junior in age, had modelled herself on Noor Jehan, the queen of music in Bombay before independence. Despite being in a profession where jealousy and backscratching are acknowledged routes to success, Lata and Noor Jehan were genuinely good friends. The friendship was so strong that they had managed to meet up at the border in the 1950s, with both sharing food they had made for each other.

Hence, it is hardly surprising that during Noor Jehan's visit, Lata sang 'Sajan ki galiyan chhod chale' from *Bazar* (1949) during a show meant to felicitate the star. This is a song Lata sang in Noor Jehan style. The composer was Shyam Sundar, who, in his short but effective tenure in cine music, created multiple milestones. One, influenced by Master Ghulam Haider, he reinforced 'Punjabiyat' (assertive robust rendition, even for female voices) in film music. Two, he gave the first break to Md. Rafi. Three, he composed a song for Lata that would become the most loved prior to the days of *Mahal*, *Andaz* or *Barsaat*. And Lata had no issues in including 'Sajan ki galiyan' in her selection. *Volume 1* also had a song composed by Shyam Sundar – 'Sun lo sajan meri baat', from *Lahore* (1949). 'Baharen phir bhi aayegi' from the same film had been sung to an international audience at the Royal Albert Hall in 1974.

'Sajan ki galiyan', composed on a mix of raag Pahadi and Manjh Khamaj, was set in time signature 7/4, in the lesser used Deepchandi taal. The orchestra found the dominance of stage instruments like the organ and cello, while the voice had an aura of *mardangi* (raw masculinity), something identified with singers of that era. This was before Lata's voice – as expressed by a member of the ISKON community in Los Angeles – sounded as pure as water falling into a forest pond. Sounding like a mix of Noor Jehan and Suraiya, the song stands out both for its tunefulness and Lata's ability to perform in the Punjabi style. Suffice it to say that Lata sounds more like her senior professionals, who were known for a stronger and grainier voice.

In a way, the lyrics were also indicative of the separation from her friend Noor Jehan, as expressed by Qamar Jalalabadi.

'Jo pass bhi unke reh na sake / Aur dard judai seh na sake'

Roughly translated, this sounds like – *Could not even stay near her/ Neither could bear the pain of separation.*

A tribute to a friend who was also a guide during Lata's initial days of playback, Lata's appreciation of the song would remain a constant feature in her interviews. Whenever any discussion on Shyam Sundar came up, she would mention this song. It is a pity that he died young, of jaundice, in 1953. He was forty-seven.[1]

Vasant Desai – soft and colourful

Song

- 'Nain so nain' (*Jhanak Jhanak Payal Baaje*, 1955)

  Lyrics: Hasrat Jaipuri

Despite being composed on a metre that resembled the staccato form, 'Sajan ki galiyan' was piercing in its heartbreaking content. The Punjabi flamboyance of eulogising hurt – something Madan Mohan also acquired in equal measure, if not more – would be omnipresent in Shyam Sundar's songs.

In complete contrast to the *Punjabiyat* was the music of Vasant Desai. Soft and relaxed, as was 'Nain so nain nahin milao', the song Lata selected from an oeuvre that included melodies like 'Main jagun re tu so jaa' (*Do Aankhen Barah Haath*, 1957), 'Dil ka khilona hai toot gaya' (*Goonj Uthi Shehnai*, 1959) and 'Jhir jhir barse sawani ankhiyan' (*Aashirwad*, 1968). 'Nain so nain' was from V. Shantaram's (1901–90) magnum opus *Jhanak Jhanak Payal Baaje* (1955), a celebration of song and dance, and, by its very concept, gave Vasant Desai full bandwidth for experimentation.

One such was scouting for musicians. Especially remarkable was his finding Shiv Kumar Sharma (1938–2022), then a folk artistc, to play for 'Nain so nain'. Filmmaker Vikash Desai, nephew of Vasant Desai, mentions[2] –

> *Well, I do not know the exact story how he found him. But it is a fact that he did search a lot for unusual instruments that had not been exposed yet. His scouting led him to get classical artistes like Pandit Samta Prasad* (tabla), *Sudarshan Adhikari* (khol), *and Shiv Kumar Sharma* (santoor, a dulcimer of Kashmiri origin, having a hundred strings to which Sharma added twenty-five more) play for the song.

V. Shantaram, the director, was destined to go the extra mile too. Vikash recounts[3] –

> *He shot the song at the famous Vrindavan Gardens in Mysore. The colours and all V Shantaram had put in the song; there was no concept of digital colouring then. It was Indigenous, the first time in the country. He was built that way; he was an 'Indian Indian'.*

He believed in India for Indians. You see, he had put everything at stake for the film. As the saying goes in Marathi – even 'shadi ke kapde' (a metaphor which translates to the clothes he wore during his marriage) were mortgaged.

I'll tell you an interesting story about the film. When it was released at Metro in Bombay, the response at the cash counter on Friday, Saturday, and Sunday was very lukewarm. The manager of Metro knew Shantaramji. He suggested that the film be taken out, or at least, the number of shows per day reduced. Shantaramji said – I will do that, post one week. And from Monday, the film picked up, to become whatever it became, with a run of seventy-five weeks.

The sudden change in public perception must have been due to word of mouth. Vikash continues[4] –

That was the conviction of Mr. Shantaram. Word of mouth is the biggest publicity. People who saw it must have felt something. It's like brewed coffee vis a vis instant coffee. Music like this, dances like this (the male lead was the dancer Gopi Krishna), take time to register. It was a combination of the visual and musical grandeur in relation to our culture. I was listening to a talk at the FTII by Mr. Roongta, the owner of Famous Cine Lab in Bombay, where he said – 'Go to your roots. If your film has something that echoes in the Ramayana or the Mahabharat or any of the Indian fables, it will create a response'.

Create a response, it did. One might go and attribute the stupendous success of the film and its music to the Indian ethos. And being the staunch nationalist Lata was, one could infer that the spirit appealed to her too. Though we could not find a documented interview where she talked specifically about the film, something in the film and its music must have prompted her to consider a song from it among her all-time favourites.

'Nain so nain', composed in raag Maalgunji with the metre in Dadra, a staple one used for dance songs, is her only duet with Hemant Kumar in the album. In fact, out of the forty-eight Lata-Hemant duets, it is the only one composed by Vasant Desai. That it topped Lata's list must be due to something special that was never spelled out in so many words by either Lata or Hemant Kumar.

Hemant Kumar, with a soft, sensitive and voluminous voice, was SD's preferred singer for Dev Anand around that time. With *Anarkali* and *Nagin* , he became the voice of Pradeep Kumar as well. While comfortable with multiple scales and especially with long notes, his Achilles heel was tackling the callisthenics necessary for Hindustani classical music and had, consequently, started taking lessons from Ali Akbar Khan during *Jhanak Jhanak Payal Baaje*.[5] Despite his limitations as a singer, Hemant was loved by music directors for his serene and magical vocal quality. He had earned Lata's love and respect not only for his singing but also for his 'brotherly stance', something that was reflected very strongly when Lata went into hiding at his Bandra flat during the Mahagujarat movement riots of 1956.[6] She was like family, and the bonding remained strong all along. Inasmuch, when actress Moushumi Chatterjee, Hemant Kumar's young daughter-in-law, liked a set of gold anklets worn by Lata, the latter immediately presented them to her.[7]

Lata, while very fond of Hemant Kumar's voice, had an even greater regard for him as a composer, and one also made it to the album. More about it in the chapter 'The Subdued Nuances'.

Notes

1 Interview with scribe Sharad Dutt in August 2014.

2 Interview with Vikash Desai over phone on 7 November 2023.

3 Ibid.

4 Ibid.

5 Bela Mukhopadhyay, *Amar Shami Hemanta* (Kolkata: Sahityam, 1999).

6 Ibid.

7 Interview with Moushumi Chatterjee on 7 April 2023.

5 The unconventional

There are composers who work hard and those who are instinctive. The next three on the list – C. Ramchandra, Salil Chowdhury and Sajjad Hussain – were gifted with the rare trait of not only composing extremely lilting melodies within a short time but also designing the blueprint for the music arrangement (intros, interludes and the like), something generally left to arrangers in Hindi cine music. These three would also mostly compose with only Lata in their minds. Not sticking to any proven formula, they would celebrate the joy of music by heading into uncharted waters and experimenting with arrangements that were novel for their time.

C. Ramchandra – music is fun

Song

- 'Mujhse mat pooch' (*Anarkali*, 1953)
  - Lyrics: Rajendra Krishan

Almost from the very beginning of her career, Lata Mangeshkar's voice had begun to exhaust the superlatives of her listeners, both musically erudite and otherwise. It was remarkable, as she had entered a world that was dominated by female singers who had grainy and thick voices. *Mardana-ang* was the patented style for ghazals, and the same was asked of filmmakers. The smoky haze was blown away once she came into her own with films like *Mahal* and *Barsaat*.

Today, such is her universal appeal that even non-Indians stumbling over her YouTube clips by chance have marvelled in the comments section at her voice. Even adversaries within her profession bow their heads in submission when it comes to her rendition that never misses a beat or is ever off-key, is flawless in its diction and pronunciation and can negotiate the most complex passages of Indian classical music.

But there is an extra dimension that made her one of the most sought-after singers during the four decades that she was most active: economics.

Those were the days of prominent composers, large ensemble orchestras and various well-appointed recording studios, and for the film's producer, these rents and wages meant hefty expenses. The orchestra instruments were real, not 'synthesized', and the recordings were live, not the spliced efforts of later years – any flub therefore meant a retake from the top for all. If the mistake was a musician's, he could be replaced or his piece could be rendered by another musician on another instrument, but what if the singer (around whom everything was woven) was error-prone? Here lay Lata's genius: her ability to pick up an entire song at short notice, not only the lyrics and tune, but the refrains, stops and gaps for orchestral interludes as well, to say nothing of embellishments and flourishes often of her own doing.

And the composer who capitalized on the economic angle the most was C. Ramchandra, aka Chitalkar Ramchandra.

In the annals of Hindi film music, C. Ramchandra's career is unique. The number of songs he composed for Lata is greater than the sum of the number of songs he composed for Asha Bhosle, Kishore Kumar, Talat Mahmood, Md. Rafi, Mahendra Kapoor (1934–2008), Shamshad Begum (1919–2013), Suraiya and himself. Lata first sang for him as the backup vocals to Geeta Dutt in 'Jawani ki rail chali jaye re' (*Shehnai*, 1947). Since then, he became completely besotted by her voice. It is said that he composed with only Lata in mind, and his career sank like the Titanic once Lata stopped singing for him. The relationship between him and Lata was more than just that of a composer-singer. She was his muse, to the extent that he was one lucky man to have witnessed Lata's historic meet up with Noor Jehan at the Wagah border.[1] Lata's trust in him was phenomenal, and right after Bhagwan's (1913–2002) *Albela,* the freak success of 1951, she had ventured into film production with *Surili,* where Bhagwan would direct, and CR would compose. This never happened.[2]

Coming to the economic angle, the word has it that nobody in the music industry could compose as fast as CR. Peer groups agreed that he could assimilate the musical essence of a sequence in a flash. He also knew the rudiments of orchestration and was open to ideas by musicians. However, despite being one of the most sought-after composers of the late 1940s through mid-1950s, his cavalier lifestyle gave him a branding that came in the way of his being bracketed as an all-time great.

Anarkali, the film for which he is remembered most, happened to him at sporadic intervals. In fact, producer S. Mukerji had him replaced twice: once because he felt that

CR was not working hard on the music (which was true, as he was majorly preoccupied with his own 1953 production, *Jhanjhar*), and the second time when he refused to work without Lata as the voice of Anarkali, the courtesan (probably fictional) betrothed to the Mughal Prince Salim. Things were so tight that he composed most of the tunes while commuting from Dadar, where he stayed, to Filmistan studios in Goregaon, a stretch of seventeen kilometers.[3] Therein lay his magic, he could internalize the requirements of the situation and create melodies to supplement the visuals almost in minutes, without resorting to the aid of any musical instrument.

Jhanjhar failed. The music, despite having a few lovely ditties like 'Ja ri ja nindiya', 'Ae pyar teri dunia se hum' and 'Chhed gayo mohe sapne mein', among others, hardly has any recall today. *Anarkali*, like the evergreen consort, has remained fresh. Lata's choice for the album – 'Mujhse mat pooch' is one of the very few early 1950s songs that continues to be part of prime time on retro channels.

Salil Chowdhury – the genius

Songs

- 'Mere Manke Diye' (*Parakh*, 1960)
  - Lyrics: Shailendra
- 'Raaton ke saaye ghane' (*Annadata*, 1972)
  - Lyrics: Yogesh

Dr Rao, who has had a personal connect with Salil Chowdhury, goes back in time:

You see, I have enjoyed the works of all music directors who worked in Hindi films, but even in my boyhood, I could identify a composition as being that of Salil Chowdhury. And this was long before I had any ideas of raags, arrangements or harmonies, such was the unique identity of his finished product.

I was fortunate to meet the man himself in the late 1990s and spoke to him at length. He was a true renaissance man skilled in writing scripts and poetry (he said that in Bengal he was considered as a respected litterateur next only to Tagore (1861–1941)), conducting choirs, in addition to composing music and playing a variety of musical instruments such as the flute, harmonium, accordion, organ, oboe, guitar and the less heard esraj. His daughter Aloka, who provided many additional inputs, remembers SD requesting him to sit in for an indisposed sound recordist for the former's own rendition of 'Ore maajhi' from *Bandini* (1963).[4]

Several music directors have acknowledged that they sought out Lata Mangeshkar any time they realized they had a splendid tune on their hands (sometimes fashioned quite by accident), even if it meant waiting for her to give a recording date. With Salil Chowdhury, this worked differently. Ever the maverick and an expert at crafting unpredictable and complex tunes, he realized that Lata was both quick on the uptake and adept in her rendition, tempting him to often challenge her with the most intricate of compositions woven deliberately with her in mind (and lose, of course). No wonder he referred to her as a once-in-a-millennium singer. Aloka remembers her being close to the family, even cooking a Maharashtrian-style fish curry during a visit home. On another occasion, she had been invited for Aloka's birthday but brought presents for all the children, having forgotten whose birthday it was![5]

However, to not include even one song of Salil would be sacrilege for Lata. Her regard for the musical genius, probably the only one who was adept at all the faculties necessary for music direction, was paramount. And she expressed it in no mean terms when she said – '*Over the course of my life I have worked with over a hundred music directors. Of these, perhaps only ten understood both music and the cinema. And of these ten, Salil was the foremost.*'[6]

Surely, she was spoilt for choice when selecting songs for the album. The typical 'problem of plenty' might have led her to overlook anything beyond the usual suspects, because of which the final choice of two songs leaves the listeners dissatisfied. Reason – while most of her 1950s through the early 1970s songs for Salil were the toast of HMV collections, she refused to look beyond the recycled corpus of some ten to fifteen oft repeated ones. One wishes she took the pain to promote something like 'Kanha bole na' (*Sangat*, 1975), a Bhajan very unusual given its symphonic nature, or a 'O re man gungun' (*Agni Pareeksha*, 1981), which, though being set in the 1980s, has elements of the best of Salil from all the previous decades. And this includes change of rhythm and tempo as well, along with the playfulness which is the hallmark of a Salil Chowdhury composition.

Unfortunately, despite having choices beyond the obvious, Lata would inevitably stick to films like *Madhumati* (1958), *Parakh* (1960), *Anand* (1970) or *Annadata* (1972). There could be a reason for the same, though. *Madhumati* was a blockbuster and difficult to ignore. *Parakh* certainly took her back to her first Bengali solo for Salil, 'Na jeona',[7] memories she has habitually recounted during her interviews. *Anand* and *Annadata* are sentimental favourites, something she found tough to sidetrack.

There could be additional reasons for Lata's deep-rooted love for *Parakh*. The story of the film was by Salil Chowdhury. Also, she sang four of the five songs in the film, and all were solos, with 'O sajna', followed by 'Mila hai kisika jhumka' as the better-known ones. 'Mere manke diye', the song she finally chose, was the only one with a sad undercurrent, a genre Salil avoided, making this number a novelty. Consequently, this magnificently understated song is less heard. Shot against a contour of light and shade created by Kamal Bose, a technique he would use in the film for 'O Sajna' as well.

The arrangement by Salil matches the picturization by director Bimal Roy. There is no perceptible percussion except a soft-touch vibraphone, and the harmonies of a choir take the song to celestial heights – yet all traffic comes to a halt when Lata sings, pure and unembellished, without a trace of echo or reverb (even the ubiquitous song violin is missing). A rare *a cappella* Hindi film song. Salil would often have a single-line instruction for Lata: he would just ask her to 'play the flute', reckoning her voice to resemble one.

* * *

Musician Kankan Dasgupta, who mostly played the accordion with Shankar Jaikishan during his tenure in Bombay, recounts this story,[8]

It was the night of Diwali, Kali Puja for Bengalis, and I was celebrating the same at the place of Samir Chowdhury, younger brother of Salil Chowdhury. I had come directly from a Shankar Jaikishan recording, and my accordion was lying in front of a garlanded picture of Goddess Kali. I wanted it to remain that way for the night.

Salil da was there too, and unfortunately, not in a great mood. Despite his monumental talent, he was not getting work. In a manner that was part cribbing and part sadness, he mentioned – you know, I have landed up with one assignment after a long time. Annadata. Hoping against hope; almost. Saying this, he suddenly asked me to pick up the accordion. I was reluctant; it was Puja time, and I wanted the instrument to attract the undivided attention of Goddess Kali. But Salil da persisted. Forced to pick up the instrument, I was asked to play a chord, followed by another, and then another. C, C minor, a few sevenths, etc. Salil da, the genius that he was, composed and arranged a full song which was going to be immortalized soon – 'Raaton ke saaye ghane'.

This song is Lata's second Salil selection. A Bengali counterpart, 'Gahan rati ghanay', in the voice of Sandhya Mukherjee, was created simultaneously. Like 'Mere man ke diye', it also has a sad tenor. Yogesh, the lyricist, wrote mostly in the mould of Shailendra, talking about the saddest and deepest thoughts in the simplest of words. If a song could be construed as a plain surface, then Salil's stamp is audible on every square inch of this one – the harmonies, chord progressions and the corkscrew tuning of the melody. Starting with the minor sixth chord, it keeps you guessing about what will be the next note and the corresponding arrangement. Something of a brain teaser, and a melodic one at that. 'Nisdin nisdin' from the same film was also like a Cretan maze, only that the Bengali version was better arranged and more popular. Stronger motive for Lata to stick to 'Raaton ke saaye'.

Sajjad Hussain – the perfectionist

Song

- 'Aaj mere naseeb mein' (*Hulchul*, 1951)
    - Lyrics: Khumar Barabankvi

A prominent feature of Lata Mangeshkar's singing was augmenting the base tune with her own interpretations. There are multiple cases where a few murkis, harkats, taans and so on, were her own. This angle was more pronounced when she sang for composers who were her juniors in the industry. With senior composers, she would restrain from offering her own inputs, though there have been instances where she pinched in, an example being during the compositional spree of 'Jao re jogi tum jao re' (*Amrapali*, 1966).[9]

However, there was one music director who wanted everything to be exactly as he had composed it. Sajjad Hussain, a multi-instrumentalist, he played the mandolin at the highest level, in the manner of classical experts, which is one of the many reasons why he was respected deeply for his profound understanding of music.

Infamous for his ego and feared for his temperament, Sajjad Hussain did only seventeen Hindi films in his entire career – apart from a few incomplete ones – as it was difficult for someone of his character to adjust to the industry. He had multiple clashes with the singers and is reputed to have coined not-so complimentary sobriquets for a few of them. Talk of political correctness!

Despite suffering from grandiose perceptions of self-worth, he held Lata in very high esteem, something surmised by his statement – 'In music, what matters most is *sur* (musical pitch). In absence of that, we say that the person is out of tune. Without sur, music has no value . . . .talking of tunefulness, Lata has no peer'.[10]

Lata revered Sajjad. He was the only one in the industry who worked without an assistant, creating tunes, writing notations and arranging the orchestra. 'Ai Dilruba nazren mila' from *Rustom Sohrab* (1963) was part of *My Favourites Volume 1*. It has been reiterated by Lata multiple times that this was her favourite Sajjad song.

'Aaj mere naseeb mein', the chosen one in *Volume 2*, is supposed to be Sajjad's favourite composition for Lata, as per scribe Raju Bharatan. Marginally based on raag Pahadi, this complex melody was Sajjad's first major hit for her. While classical music was Sajjad's forte, he could dovetail the nuances with light tunes and keep the phrases short, so they would fit into the structure of a film song.

However, Sajjad, with his very limited output, could at best be termed as a boutique composer, given the fact that his peers did at least five times more work for the cinema. What would have happened had Sajjad been a tad diplomatic and the industry kinder?

It is difficult to tell. Maybe the law of averages would have caught up. Or there might have been many more 'Aaj mere Naseeb mein' and 'Ai Dilruba nazren milas'. But given his consistent track record, he surely would have inspired many more composers, and one of them is part of the next chapter.[11]

Notes

1 Per C. Ramchandra's autobiography, the meeting happened in 1953. Some news reports mention the year as 1951.

2 Dilip Shripad Phansalkar, *The Bitter-Sweet Cocktail – Movies, Wine, Women – The Life of C Ramachandra* (Lansing, MI: Professor Toofaanii Publishers, 2023).

3 Ibid, and Dr Mandar Bichu, *Lata: Voice of the Golden Era* (Mumbai: Popular Prakashan, 2010).

4 Interview with Aloka Nanjappa over the phone in November 2023.

5 Ibid.

6 www.salilda.com. Original source: *Aalokpaat* magazine, November 1997 issue (page 8). Translated from Bengali by Gautam Choudhury.

7 'O Sajna', a famous song from *Parakh* (1960) was based on 'Na Jeona'.

8 Interview with Kankan Dasgupta over phone on 2 December 2023.

9 Dinesh Chandra Shailendra, https://thesongpedia.com/story-behind-the-making-of-jao-re-jogi-tum-jao-re-amrapali.

10 Nasreen Munni Kabir, *Lata in Her Own Voice* (London: Hyphen Films, for Channel Four, 1990).

11 Madan Mohan was inspired by Sajjad's 1952 song 'Yeh hawa ye raat ye chandni' from *Sangdil* to create 'Tujhe kya sunau main dilruba' (*Aakhri Dao*, 1958).

6 The tearful craving

Madan Mohan was someone who composed with only Lata in mind. And it was his army training that helped create a feel that was polished and sophisticated. One is not sure if it was by design or chance, but his compositions had a lot of sadness, giving rise to the feeling of tearful craving . . .

Madan Mohan – closest to the heart

Songs

- 'Zara si aahat hoti hai' (*Haqueeqat*, 1964)
  - Lyrics: Kaifi Azmi
- 'Rasm-e-ulfat' (*Dil ki Rahen*, 1973)
  - Lyrics: Naqsh Lyallpuri

The opening lines on the website for Madan Mohan that is run by his family quote him as having said,

> *In composing tunes, my concentration is focused on the melodic content of the song. I have always believed that melody is the soul of a song and a simple tune, typically Indian in form, with melody as its predominant feature, always reaches deep into the hearts of the listeners. You have supported me in my belief by making such songs your favourites.*[1]

The repeated emphasis on the word melody has a strong connect with the music of Madan Mohan. However, the mention of 'simple tune' seems out of place. At least in his songs for Lata. They were anything but simple. They were heavy and ornate, with an omnipresent melancholic aura. You associated a sense of pain, of emotional friction, even in the 'happy' romantic songs. The Madan Mohan – Lata Mangeshkar partnership was destined to make you cry without sounding mushy. A separate genre if there was any within the 'romantic Hindi film song', something unilaterally agreed upon by the composing fraternity, including Naushad, RD and O. P. Nayyar, among others.

Madan Mohan passed away in 1975 at the age of fifty-one. To contextualise the lingering impact of the genre, we need to appreciate that even after almost fifty years, during which attitudes, expressions and yardsticks of excellence have undergone multiple changes, the Madan Mohan – Lata combo remains like a signature tune epitomising 'tearful craving'. No wonder, multiple compilations like 'Lata sings for Madan Mohan' have been published through the years, happening much before Lata set to choose her favourites.

Given the basic constraint that most of the songs had already been released and recycled in albums of assorted colours and rpm speeds, one guesses that Lata must have had a tough time selecting her favourites. That there were 227 songs for her to select from does not make things easy.[2] One assumes she was not sure where to start.

The eternal conflict between Baby Boomers and Gen X continues here too. The former labelled her 1950s work with Madan Mohan as the best. However, Lata's propensity to perform 'Lag ja gale' and 'Naina basre', both from Madan Mohan's first silver jubilee film *Woh Kaun Thi?* (1964), gives us the feeling that her favourites were songs of the 1960s. It is the popularity of these songs, along with other crowd favourites like 'Yun hasraton ke daag' (*Adalat*, 1958) and 'Aap ki nazron ne samjha' (Anpadh, 1962), that shifts the period to the late 1950s through the mid-1960s, times when her voice was at its most well-rounded.

Talking of *Woh Kaun Thi?*, Madan Mohan had expected to be bestowed with the Filmfare award for Best Music Director for the film. Per Lata, some people claiming to have the capability to influence the jury met him, demanding money in exchange for the award, only to be turned down. One does not know whether it was the result of his refusal to compromise on his principles, but the award was given to Laxmikant Pyarelal for their score in *Dosti* (1964). His expectations were belied; Madan Mohan was dejected. When Lata went up to him and expressed her sorrow over the fact, the self-respecting man had said, 'The fact that you felt sad for this is an award of which I am proud.'[3]

This stance does not condemn the quality of the music of *Dosti*, one of the finest albums of composers Laxmikant and Pyarelal. However, if given the opportunity to select only one composer of 1964, it is difficult to look beyond Madan Mohan. His films that year, in alphabetical order, were – *Aap ki Parchhaiyan, Gazal, Jahan Ara, Pooja ke Phool, Sharabi, Suhagan* and *Woh Kaun Thi?* Each of these films had songs that became iconic with time, and not just on account of nostalgia. All of them barring, *Sharabi*, had at least one song of Lata that remains a favourite with music lovers.

One film that missed the Filmfare list in 1964 was *Haqueeqat*. Censored in 1964, it was released in January 1965, with the music receiving raving reviews. With a plot about the Sino-Indian War, the film was shot with Ladakh as the background. While most of the scenes were created indoors by art director M. S. Sathyu,[4] director Chetan Anand took his cast and crew to shoot on India's highest plateau. High altitude, low oxygen, freezing air and so on, would create an ambiance that was warlike. And the music, including the background score, followed the director's vision. Not much of a surprise here, as Madan Mohan was a second lieutenant of the British-India army during Second World War. His knowledge of the struggles of soldiers in valleys where silence was occasionally broken by funnelled sound waves and echoes was based on experience.

Madan Mohan's personal favourite of the three Lata solos from *Haqueeqat* was 'Khelo na mere dil se'. The song was left out of the film, and we do not know the situation for which this was composed; it could have been when the lovers Captain Bahadur Singh (Dharmendra) and Anagmo (Priya Rajvansh (1936–2000)) were in the initial phase of dating. Listeners should be grateful to Lata for her indulgence in 'Khelo na mere dil se', which she popularized through shows among a younger generation not exposed to the song, including her concert at the Royal Albert Hall in 1979, this time with the Wren Orchestra.

In total contrast to the almost linear and haunting affair that was 'Khelo na mere dil se', 'Zara si aahat', the song that featured in *Volume 2*, is typical of Madan Mohan of the mid-late 1950s. A time when, as a composer growing in stature, his focus was more on using Hindustani classical to colour his songs. Hence, it is hardly any surprise that 'Zara si aahat' is composed in two raags. Primarily. Yaman Kalyan in the refrain, and Kedar in the paragraph (antara). Point to note – both Yaman Kalyan and Kedar are part of the same 'thaat' (scale) in Hindustani classical music – Kalyan, hence, the mix sounds organic.

'Zara si aahat' also reminds us of a few stories recounted by Lata, which, roughly translated, would be something like this,[5]

> *Madan 'Bhaiya' (brother) had learnt Classical music, and extensively heard eminent singers too. He used to sing and had a well-trained voice. Reason his compositions, which included geets, ghazals or bhajans were so effective. He was a complete artiste. And very tuneful too.*
>
> *During rehearsals, he used to keep on singing. And ask me to select whatever I liked from the plethora of tunes he was singing. Flabbergasted, I would reply that this was a nigh impossible task; remembering all that he sang and reproducing the same during recording was beyond my capability. At times he would go on humming a taan continuously, not paying any heed to my attempts at interruption. After some time, he used to take it easy and tell me – well, now let me sing properly and teach you the song.*
>
> *He was a great music director. Nobody could match him when it was creating ghazals.*

Another probable reason Lata chose this song could have been her admiration for raag Yaman/Kalyan.[6] It is also rumoured that she mastered the style of rolling the notes (the part 'Sochta hai' in 'Zara si aahat' is an example) after listening to Bade Ghulam Ali Khan.

* * *

The 1970s found Madan Mohan integrating western forms into his songs. A preference for harmonic arrangements, and onboarding new musicians like Bhupinder Singh (1940–2022) whose twelve-string guitar became a regular. Or recording at the Film Center Studio which was like the second home to composer RD. Every studio has its own acoustics, and the setup there helped in creating a very layered sound.

Despite the change of style, Hindustani classical remained his preferred choice, and one finds the sitar occupying the place of pride in his arrangements. Madan Mohan was not only a huge fan of sitar exponent Vilayat Khan (1928–2004), but he was also a friend, despite the inside joke that Madan would be inspired by Vilayat's musical phrases to create his tunes.[7] By the mid-1960s, the sitar had become an inseparable part of Madan Mohan's orchestra. Vilayat, by that time, had become somewhat of a phenomenon. From the late 1950s, he hardly played for the cinema, but Rais Khan (1939–2017), his nephew, became a regular with Madan Mohan. And Lata Mangeshkar loved it when he played the sitar in her songs. As it was in the case of 'Rasm-e-Ulfat', the second song of Madan Mohan in *Volume 2*.

This song was based on *Madhuvanti*, a raag popularized mostly by Vilayat Khan. The phrasing of the song was like a sitar recital. The interludes were mostly about the sitar, and the song concluded with a *jhala*. To make it believable, Rakesh Pandey, the male lead, is seen playing the sitar portions in the song.

Rehana Sultan, the actress, opens her mouth, enunciating the words properly; in effect, she carries them well.

* * *

All this while Madan Mohan was competing with fresh blood . . . the trailblazers of the 1970s.

Notes

1 www. Madanmohan.in.

2 Dr Mandar Bichu, Lata – *Voice of the Golden Era* (Mumbai: Popular Prakashan, 2010).

3 www. Madanmohan.in.

4 M. S. Sathyu's interview in the Filmfare, Awards issue, May 1966.

5 www. Madanmohan.in.

6 Op Cit, 'The Classicists', Notes #2.

7 Namita Devidayal, *The Sixth String of Vilayat Khan* (Chennai: Westland, 2018).

7 The trailblazers – II

If Shankar Jaikishan (and to some extent O. P. Nayyar, who never composed for Lata) was the toast of the radio dial chaser and the jukebox in the 1960s, RD and the duo of Laxmikant and Pyarelal were by far the busiest composers of the decade of the 1970s. And they too would consider composing for Lata something close to their hearts.

Rahul Dev Burman – the modernist

Songs

- 'Kya Jaanu Sajan' (*Baharon ke Sapne*, 1967)
    - Lyrics: Majrooh Sultanpuri
- 'Baahon Mein Chale Aao' (*Anamika*, 1973)
    - Lyrics: Majrooh Sultanpuri
- 'Panna ki Tamanna' (*Heera Panna*, 1973)
    - Lyrics: Anand Bakshi
    - Co-singer: Kishore Kumar

While discussing the compositions of RD for Lata Mangeshkar, we were in a dilemma when it came to choosing the representative Lata-RD song of the 1960s. It was not that the choices were many. RD had only released eleven films from

1960 through 1969. The number of published Lata Mangeshkar songs was seventeen (a few more were published later, in the 2020s). In an era when she would normally have an average of two or three solos in a film, this was low.

The problem was that at least fourteen of the seventeen songs were of the highest quality.

Lata's chosen one from the 1960s in *Volume 2* was about love and pain, the coexistence of which has often been a definitive template for the romantic solo in Hindi cinema. And while using C minor as the scale for 'Kya Jaanu Sajan', RD also used the B note fleetingly along with the accepted B flat note, a trait that corresponds to the Khamaj thaat (scale) in Hindustani classical music. RD would gradually evolve as an expert in using the same.

The song has a fascinating history. For decades, it had been known as a duet between Lata Mangeshkar and her sister Usha Mangeshkar (born 1935). This was because one hears two voices simultaneously – for certain portions in the song. Around that time, RD was trying to put together a technique that could be leveraged for twin-track recordings.[1] Song recordings then used to happen on spools. The equipment had an erasing head and a recording head side by side, and any recording would be preceded by wiping off whatever was on the spool. For this song, RD first got Lata to sing the melody. Next, he asked her to sing the harmonies at a few earmarked places and recorded them on the same spool. This time, he had removed the erasing head. Hence, both the melody and the harmony, though sung by the same person, are heard concurrently. In 1966, this was something very innovative. RD repeated the method again with 'Baithe hain kya unke pass' in *Jewel Thief* (1967).

RD had spoken to the media about the experimentation. But GCI, the company that owned the rights to the record, took no notice. It was only after Lata mentioned it to the press in the first decade of the twenty-first century that the record was amended.

The filming of the song has a history that is no less absorbing. Nasir Husain (1926–2002), the director, who was also producing *Teesri Manzil* (1966), had set up the set of a village fair with a Ferris wheel in a suburb of Bombay. A particular song, 'Dekhiye Sahibon', was being shot there by director Vijay Anand. The shoot would happen during the day, and the same set was to be used for 'Kya Jaanu Sajan' after 9.00 p.m. *Teesri Manzil* was a colour film, while *Baharon ke Sapne* was in black and white. To reuse the existing raw stock, 'Kya Jaanu Sajan' was planned in colour. This was a dream sequence, hence a detour from the raw reality in the lives of the young lovers.

Unfortunately, the results were not encouraging, and the song had to be reshot inside the studio. The introduction and the ending of the song, which had been shot in black and white at the location, were retained.

Lata's second selection is among her most admired songs of the 1970s. From a Ferris wheel to a cast iron swing on a veranda, from melancholic but dreamy evenings to an impish nightcap, it was a 180-degree turn.

* * *

One of Lata Mangeshkar's most talked-about shows was the one at the Royal Albert Hall in 1974. She was the first Indian artiste of popular music to sing there. While the request to perform at the hallowed venue was greeted with scepticism by the authorities, the cash registers at the booking counter told a different story. The album sleeve recounts the same:

> *Seldom, indeed, has the hall been booked for a single recitalist three times in one week. What, however, made the event equally unique was to have the hall packed by an oriental artiste for all the three nights – and something more. For even after the intermission on the final night (March 14), there still were crowds willing to pay double the highest price for admission to the hall!*[2]

In this show, Lata's first concert abroad, the only RD song featured was 'Baahon Mein Chale Aao'. *Anamika*, the popular thriller with a Hitchcockian feel, had a good run at the theatres in India. However, 'Baahon Mein Chale Aao', a song that had a very liberated feeling around it, was considered ahead of its time. Gradually, the song became iconic, with Jaya Bhaduri, the lead, who lip-synched it on the screen, also promoting it.

But the strongest promotional activity was Lata Mangeshkar's. In the concert, this was her third song, after a customary sloka and 'Inhi logon ne' (*Pakeezah*, 1972). The applause was overwhelming.

By the late 1960s, romance bordering on playfulness had a good following in India. While this genre has been considered the forte of her sister Asha Bhosle, Lata Mangeshkar too sang a few that were immensely popular during their time. But 'Baahon Mein Chale Aao' has had a life far beyond the ephemeral popularity inflated by programmes like 'Binaca Geetmala' (a popular radio show), where it struggled to find a place in the final countdown and made it to the thirty-sixth spot then. Today, fifty years hence, it might top a popularity chart. This 4/4 composition, which has a lilt comparable to the waltz, a 3/4 movement, remains close to our hearts.

The intriguing part of the E major scale song is the use of the passing notes – flat third and flat sixth. Also, RD might have used a dyad, a two-note chord combining E and B, in the beginning. One can go back in time and find an analogy in the SD composition that was arranged by RD, 'Roop tera mastana' (*Aradhana*, 1969), where two notes, the first and fifth notes of the C scale, play key roles.

Similar templates for songs of seduction? Not really. 'Roop tera mastana' was a song in a male voice. It was more demanding. 'Baahon Mein Chalo Aao' was more soothing. Good-humoured. And certainly, more comforting. The use of short phrases of humming by Lata Mangeshkar also added to the intensely playful spirit.

Part of the song was shot in Sur Mandir, RD's bungalow on 15th Road, Khar, Bombay. The composition happened in 1971, and the tune was first used in the background of the 1971 film *Caravan*, which, like *Anamika*, was produced by Tahir Husain (1938–2010, Nasir Husain's younger brother and father of contemporary actor and filmmaker Aamir Khan). Pandit Hariprasad Chaurasia played the tune on the flute for the background score. In *Anamika*, the song was artfully arranged with the conga, the dugi, a prominent string section, the bass guitar and the twelve-string guitar.

Bhupinder Singh's twelve-string guitar would play a significant role in the third and last song Lata chose from her repertoire of songs for RD.

* * *

'Panna ki Tamanna', the third song in the selection, was composed by RD during the phase of separation from his wife Rita Patel in 1972. He had shifted to Caesar's Palace Hotel (now defunct), Khar, Bombay. Suffering from depression, he was unable to work until friends got him back on his feet. And Dev Anand was among the few who inspired him, hijacking the tune of 'Panna ki Tamanna' the moment RD played it on his harmonium. A duet between Lata and Kishore Kumar, this is also the seventh and second last duet in *My Favourites Volume 2*.

Zeenat Aman, the lead of the film, was ecstatic when she heard about the song. In her previous film, *Hare Rama Hare Krishna* (1971), though she was the central character, she was the hero's (Dev Anand's) sister. Here, she would play Panna, and her name would not only be part of the title, but it would also be there in a song. Subsequently, her blow-ups were everywhere. By the time the film received the censor certificate on 15 November 1973, she had become a star. Both Dev and Zeenat were at Fish Tail Lodge in Pokhara, shooting for *Ishk Ishk Ishk* then.[3]

Unfortunately, the film was so weak that despite the star image of Dev Anand and the oomph of Zeenat, it struggled to break even. The film's claim, apart from the Vauxhall Victor Estate car with stickers of country names all over the body, was the Hasselblad camera – the brand was suddenly famous after it was used to take photos on the moon – that Dev was seen to carry during a few sequences. And a Houdini act where Dev produces a multi-coloured bikini out of thin air, leading to a photo shoot – with Zeenat in a hammock – that made it to the centrespreads of films magazines.

Thankfully, the songs, especially this one, became the redeeming feature of the film. During the premiere shows at metros, the albums would be auctioned by Dev Anand and customers would willingly pay INR 1,000 or more during times when LP records would be priced around INR 40–50. Today, YouTube hits are in millions, even though the song has often been removed from the video sharing platform, resulting in fresh uploads that are not very old.

This song was among Dev Anand's personal favourites as well, given the fact that he had specifically talked about the filming in his autobiography, *Romancing with Life*.[4]

Lata, a cinephile, was fond of a host of actors, from Yul Brynner to Cary Grant. And Dev Anand was a favourite too, if not for anything else, for his good looks, and she would consider his being at song sessions a pleasurable experience.[5]

Dev would remember Lata thus[6] – 'Lata Mangeshkar was among my most admired singers from the time Kishore Kumar and I would take the night local train back home, moving from studio to studio in search of work.'

Kishore Kumar later became like family. On his birthday, he would often visit Lata's place early in the morning and then vanish for the day. Media shy and elusive, he gave one of the most well-known interviews to Lata Mangeshkar at the Watergate Hotel, Washington, DC, in the first week of June in 1985. And despite being in an industry where bitterness and backbiting rule, Lata's relationship with RD was also like family. He called her Didi (elder sister), and Lata often spoke to RD in his native, Bengali.[7] She was also an admirer of his command over the rhythm section and mentioned the same in multiple interviews. Given her view of RD's style, it is intriguing to note that none of the songs she chose highlighted his grasp over the mixing of rhythms. On the contrary, these were songs of the sweetest variety, the last two being happy ones. It could be that is how she identified with her brother-in-law (RD married Asha Bhosle), who would remind her of some halcyon and joyful moments in her life.[8]

Laxmikant Pyarelal – the born survivors

Songs

- 'Kareeb aa yeh nazar' (*Anita*, 1967)
  - Lyrics : Raja Mehedi Ali Khan
- 'Jaane kyon log mohobbat' (*Mehboob ki Mehndi*, 1971)

  Lyrics : Anand Bakshi

RD, one of the trailblazers of the 1970s, was family. The equally prolific Laxmikant Kudalkar and Pyarelal Sharma, jointly known as Laxmikant Pyarelal, or just L-P, were more than family. They were Lata's protégés, the relationship extending beyond music sittings and recordings. Lata's association with this composing duo was so long and profound, and their songs together so numerous, that Pyarelal (the surviving member) finds it difficult to recall precisely when and where he saw her first.[9] As young boys barely into their teens, both were already part of the industry's instrumental accompanists (Laxmikant playing the mandolin and Pyarelal the violin) when Lata Mangeshkar formed a 'Sureela Bal Kala

Kendra' involving them, Pyarelal's brother Ganesh, as well as her own siblings, sister Usha and (leading the team) brother Hridaynath.

Thus, nurtured by her, they progressed from musicians to arrangers to assistant music directors to independent music directors, all the while in the shade of her protection. Pyarelal acknowledges this enormous debt to this day – not only did they get to work with one of the finest singers of the millennium then at the peak of her talent, but they also benefited from the enormous power and influence she wielded in the industry as she championed their cause.[10]

Songs from their first released film, *Parasmani* (1963), achieved much popularity and many offers poured in, but these were mostly low-budget 'stunt' films from smaller banners. (Indian films of the time were broadly classifiable into definite categories such as 'costume drama', 'religious/mythological' and 'stunt' (which were given to a preponderance of fight sequences), and the broadest catch-all basket, the 'social'. There was no 'musical' because *every* film was a musical.

By the advent of the 1960s, Lata Mangeshkar was a major star and a force to reckon with in the industry, a fact of which she was fully aware. She commanded a higher price and, with rare exceptions, sang only in films helmed by A-list producers and composers and those that featured only the top actors and actresses of the time (an actress had truly 'arrived' when she had lip-synced to a Lata song).

But to help the struggling duo of Laxmikant and Pyarelal, an indulgent Lata agreed to sing in 'B' grade films that were the first to come their way. Almost all their first twenty-odd films were in black and white and were mostly based on Indian epics or featured brawny heroes like Dara Singh (1928–2012) (India's Steve Reeves) – and all featured songs by Lata Mangeshkar. As a result, not only did the films assume a dignity not usually associated with their genre, but in corollary a slew of less-known actresses like Bela Bose, Nishi, Uma Bhende and yet-to-be-heroine Mumtaz all got to 'sing' a Lata Mangeshkar song.

Once they had signed their first big banner colour films, which had major lead actors (Filmyug's *Aaye Din Bahar Ke* (1966) and Chitralaya's *Pyar Kiye Jaa* (1966)), the floodgates opened. Very soon they had signed up for more than a dozen films and were so swamped with work and pressured by deadlines, they had problems getting dates from the equally busy Lata Mangeshkar. Pyarelal recalls Lata's annoyance at having to adjust her own schedule, telling him on one occasion, 'I have an 11:30 a.m. sitting with Shankar-Jaikishan tomorrow in the same studio. If you can finish your recording between 10 and 11 a.m., only then I'll do it.'[11]

The next morning, following a hasty tweaking down of the tune's complexity, the song was recorded.

Except Geeta Dutt, L-P worked with all the major playback singers of the time, but their reverence for Lata is tangible in their songs for her. At times she would be given a separate catchphrase during the entry, for example, in 'Shaam dhale jamuna kinare' (*Pushpanjali*, 1970). There were instances where the orchestra would be muted at her entry ('Krishna Krishna', from *Naya Din Nai Raat* (1974)) or her stanza in a duet would be tuned differently from that of her co-singer ('Kaise jeete hain bhala', from *Dost* (1974)). Many of the *murkis* and *harkats* were her own doing and sometimes she would suggest some alteration or addition to a tune. For example, in the song 'Meghwa gagan beech jhanke' (*Harishchandra Taramati* (1963), having the last syllable 'ke' of the line *Payal jhanjhanake* land on a *madhyam* note (even though the song's Kalavati raag conventionally excludes it) was her doing. She too has gone on record to name 'Jeevan dor tumhi sang bandhi' (*Sati Savitri* (1964)) and the title song of *Satyam Shivam Sundaram* as being among her favourite L-P compositions.

However, her choice of the two songs from L-P's oeuvre in *Volume 2* appears to have been done in haste. These are not the automatic picks of a connoisseur. Any compilation entitled 'My Favourites', especially one drawn up by the artiste herself, becomes a statement of opinion and is therefore beyond argument. Still, given her voluminous body of work for L-P, one ponders over the selection, given that no other music director has embellished her songs with such a variety of *thekas* (rhythm patterns), raags and genres or displayed her voice with a level of respect that borders on reverence. The number of songs she sang for L-P is over 700, offering her a spectrum wide enough to choose from.

A probable reason for our dissatisfaction is a mismatch of expectations. 'Kareeb aa yeh nazar phir mile na mile', the first L-P song in the album, is from the last of the three 'suspense trilogy' films by Raj Khosla (1925–91) with Sadhana (1941–2015) in the female lead. The first film of the three, *Woh Kaun Thi?* borrowed liberally from "The Woman in White" with a touch of *Vertigo* (1958) towards the end. The second was *Mera Saaya* (1966) and the third (from which the song in discussion is taken) was *Anita*. In all three, Sadhana played a mysterious (possibly ghostly) woman recurrently appearing to the lovestruck and confused hero. In all three films, the arrival of her character (or characters) on the screen was heralded by a haunting song penned by lyricist Raja Mehdi Ali Khan. (Only for *Anita* Raj Khosla, for some reason, eschewed regular composer Madan Mohan in favour of L-P.)

But this song in *Anita* isn't a recurring ghost song, but one that beseeches the hero to come close to her because there's no telling if the opportunity will arise again. In this respect, the words closely mirror another *Woh Kaun Thi?* song, 'Lag ja gale', which, in comparison, is undeniably superlative in every department, to the extent that this *Anita* song today remains near obliterated. To the extent that one might feel that it has been forcefully fitted simply to get the buy-in of distributors. And while the tune does have a haunting feel, the rhythm is monotonous and does not help in letting the song grow on the listener. Not even Lata's promotion of the same helped.

* * *

The same logic does not extend to 'Jaane kyon log mohabbat kiya karte hain', though. Based on a mix of raags Shivranjani and Madhuvanti, there is something very innocent and intense about the tune and the lyrics that touches the listener. The song has multiple phrases, including a mukhra that sounds like a *shayari* – a standalone stanza before the song. For a change, it has short interludes. The antara does sound a bit convoluted, though, and one loses the hummable factor that is strong for the mukhra.

Mehboob ki Mehndi (a 'Muslim social', in Bollywood parlance) opens with the heroine Shabana (played by Leena Chandavarkar) rendering the song in a competition.

Anand Bakshi's lyrics tell of the futility of love and the pain of heartbreak, a portent of events to come in Shabana's own life. Lata Mangeshkar's liking of the song does not seem to be limited to its inclusion in this compilation. For a live concert in 2002, she had her younger sister Usha render it, who was game enough to do so (given that she had a sizeable repertoire of her own to choose from) and did a competent job of it. Perhaps Lata felt that the song gelled well with the milieu of the show's Hyderabad location and its Urdu-speaking audience. One can also find the use of short phrases that are reminiscent of Afghan music that help sustain the Islamic flavour. Unfortunately, the dholaks (a variety of the Indian drums) drown out much of the instrumental music that includes fillers and obligatos on the swarmandal (harp) and the flute.

While respecting Lata's choice, one wishes she had included a few uncluttered ones, a discretion she had exercised for *Volume 1*. While there was no 'O ghata saanwari' (*Abhinetri*, 1970), 'Yeh raat bhi jaa rahi hai' (*Sau Saal Baad*, 1966) and 'Woh hain zara khafa khafa' (*Shagird*, 1967), the chosen two in *Volume 1* had strong serenity indexes.

However, maybe to add variety to the album, Lata picked a few of the calm and composed variety as well, as we recount in the next chapter.

Notes

1 Anirudha Bhattacharjee and Balaji Vittal, *R. D. Burman, The Man the Music* (Noida: Harper Collins India, 2011).

2 Album sleeve of 'Lata Mangeshkar: Live at Royal Albert Hall, London', The Gramophone Company of India Limited, production date 1978.

3 Interview with Arun Sharma, sound recordist, on 10 October 2020.

4 Dev Anand, *Romancing with Life* (New Delhi: Penguin India, 2007).

5 Yatindra Mishra, *Lata Sur Gatha* (New Delhi: Vani Prakashan, 2016).

6 'Aalokpaat', November 1997.

7 Interview with singer-musician Shurjo Bhattacharya in 2010 – by Anirudha Bhattacharjee.

8 RD was married to Asha Bhosle, Lata Mangeshkar's sister.

9 Interview of Pyarelal Sharma by Chandrashekhar Rao in November 2023.

10 Ibid.

11 Ibid.

8 The subdued nuances

As an industry, pre-millennium Hindi cine music catered to a very wide variety of listeners, ranging from devout classical lovers to Gen Y kids brought up on a diet of strong anti-establishment messages. Unfortunately, with time, clutter became an essential component in music, and styles once steeped in tradition were reworked to disco beats, making for a painful hearing experience. On the flip side, there were composers who considered uncluttered simplicity a strong virtue. Old-timers would immediately associate the trait with the compositions of Hemant Kumar, Khayyam and Ghulam Mohammed. Rajesh Roshan was another composer whose songs gave the feeling that he was at great peace with himself. This is surprising, as he started his career in the 1970s.

Hemant Kumar – friendly notes

Song

- 'O Bekaraar Dil' (*Kohraa*, 1964)
    - Lyrics: Kaifi Azmi

Much is known and will be remembered of Hemanta Kumar Mukherjee, aka Hemant Kumar, for his sonorous renditions of light songs, both for the cinema and off it. Salil Chowdhury had classified his voice, which was a mix of tenor and baritone, as God's own. The pearly purity in his tone led Ms Mangeshkar to equate his renditions with that of a sage. His near-godly aura also played a role in creating the perception of a saint who had, by mistake, landed in the big, imperfect world of cine music.

One might note that while Hemant Kumar's accomplishment as a singer has never been in doubt, his work as a composer has largely remained unappreciated by the casual followers of Hindi cinema. His stature as a singer was so big that it overshadowed his success as a composer.

Lata Mangeshkar has, however, been kind to Hemant Kumar, the music director, identifying with his well-groomed tunes with all her heart. He was like extended family, and it was a result of his doggedness that she sang for S. Mukerji in *Anandmath* (1952) and *Anarkali* and followed it up with *Nagin* after the studio owner had turned her down in *Shaheed* (1948). It was also at his insistence that she came back to singing after a prolonged hiatus that happened courtesy of a painful bout of sinusitis. It was in June 1961, with 'Kahin Deep Jale Kahin Dil', composed by Hemant Kumar from the first Hindi film he produced – *Bees Saal Baad (1962)*. She did not take any money for the song, and was specially acknowledged in the film's credit roll

Her selection of 'O Bekaraar Dil' from *Kohraa* (1964) also justifies the virtues Hemant Kumar's music stood for: soft, simple, light and extremely pleasing to the ear. This is also a rare case of a Hindi song with a *sanchari*, an elusive phrase connecting two *antaras*. A form that is part of the *Dhrupad* system, it finds wide application in the songs of Rabindranath Tagore. Hemant Kumar, one of the pioneers of the genre, used it in a manner most appropriate. Kaifi Azmi's lyrics, 'Aaye ghata phir se ghata chhaye, Aaur pyaasi kali gham ki jali taras taras jaye', seem to have been written deliberately to create the imagery of deceit. A kind of literary device: when a poem's subject's 'joy' cup runneth over, their wishes turn negative to thwart the evil eye, just as in India, a beautiful woman or child has a small black spot applied to the unblemished face or a sculptor deliberately chips a piece off a small toe if a statue has turned out impossibly perfect.

Incidentally, the song was from a film also produced by Hemant Kumar. And his darkest one, where Alfred Hitchcock's *Rebecca* (1940) found its Indian adaptation with the additional baggage of five songs, of which three were huge hits. 'O Bekaraar Dil' was one of them. The film, made by Biren Naug, failed.

Biren Naug (1922–64), who was Hemen Gupta's (1914–67) import from Calcutta, made a name for himself as an art director after collaborating with stalwarts like Guru Dutt (1925–64) and Vijay Anand. *Bees Saal Baad* (1962), his version of *The Hound of the Baskervilles*, was a monumental success. *Kohraa* disappointed. A dejected Hemant Kumar, who had received an invitation to travel to the West Indies, started planning for the trip and invited Naug to accompany him. Naug refused. By the time Hemant Kumar came back from the successful tour, the songs of *Kohraa* had become extremely popular. Naug passed away a few days later due to a stomach ulcer. He was forty-two.[1]

Khayyam – poetic feel
Songs

- 'Baharon Mera Jeevan Bhi Sanwaro' (*Aakhri Khat*, 1966)
    - Lyrics: Kaifi Azmi
- 'Apne Aap Raaton Mein' (*Shankar Husain*, 1977)
    - Lyrics: Kaif Bhopali
- 'Dikhai Diye Yun' (*Bazaar*, 1982)
    - Lyrics: Mir Taqi Mir

When our initial exercise started with comparing the song list of *My Favourites – Volume 1 & 2*, we were pleasantly surprised to find composer Khayyam represented with three songs in *Volume 2* as compared to 'Aap Yun Faaslon Se' (*Shankar Husain*, 1977) and 'Ai dil-e-nadaan' (*Razia Sultan*, 1983) in *Volume 1*. More so, because from Khayyam's trademark languorous style to composing for the poetry of the Mughal era, it was all there.

The first Khayyam composition in *Volume 2* is sans any surprise. 'Baharon Mera Jeevan Bhi Sanwaro' is the most well-known Khayyam-Lata song of the 1960s. This song, written by Kaifi Azmi, is to the ear what a meal of ambrosia and nectar prepared by celestial beings and served by Aphrodite herself would be to the palate. This song also ended a small misunderstanding between the composer and the singer, meaning Lata was singing for Khayyam after some time.

While it features A-Team talents, its principal musicians too sport impeccable credentials: Shiv Kumar Sharma on the santoor, Hariprasad Chaurasia on the flute and Rais Khan on the sitar, all accomplished classical musicians.

An introduction lasting more than a minute, unusually long for a film song, in Khayyam's Pahadi raag sets the tone. One can almost see the sun rising in the Kulu Valley in sync with that long and languid flute piece. It ends with three descending notes, the third one landing on the 'sam' (first beat of the rhythm). This is signature Khayyam stuff; three piano notes being used similarly (with an effect just as arresting) to start his duet, 'Jeet hi lenge baazi hum tum' from *Shola Aur Shabnam* (1961) several years earlier.

On the screen, a maiden (played by Indrani Mukherjee) seeks benediction from nature to send her a loving life partner. She assumes she is alone in the valley, unaware that a young man (Rajesh Khanna) has been drawn to her voice. Hindi films of that era are replete with that voice-first scenario setting up a hero/heroine meeting, almost always the voice being that of Lata Mangeshkar.

Her rendition here is relaxed, the long flowing notes caressing the lyrics and fading out well into the interspersed 'gayaki' (singing) notes of Rais Khan's sitar.

Like so many other songs from Hindi cinema's classic era, this one too has transcended the needs of the on-screen situation for which it was composed and taken on a life of its own. Little did producer-director Chetan Anand envisage that *Aakhri Khat*, which later became famous as Rajesh Khanna's first censored film (and the second to be released), would mostly be remembered down the ages for a song then considered inconsequential. The reason Anand made the film was to capture the reactions of the pedestrians to a toddler (Bunty Behl) moving around the streets unaided, with Jal Mistry (1923–2000) following him with a handheld ARRI-2 camera.

** ** **

'Apne Aap Raaton Mein', another Pahadi based composition and the second Khayyam-Lata song in the album has an engaging story too. Madhuchhanda Chakrabarty, the near-forgotten leading lady recounts the same in an interview with the authors.[2]

> You see, both the songs of Lata Mangeshkar from *Shankar Husain* had been previously recorded by in the voice of a very well-known singer.[3] I think this happened in the 1960s. Kamal Amrohi Sahib (1918–1993) got the songs re-recorded in the voice of Lata Mangeshkar. Being the character who would lip-synch the songs, I was doubly pleased and was there at the recording which happened at Mehboob studios. Lata Mangeshkar's voice was like a boon, and I felt shattered when she passed away a month ago. Some people should not die. Wish she could have lived five hundred years.
>
> The song was picturised in Valsad, a small town in Gujarat. It was shot at night, as I play a sleepwalker in the film. Being the perfectionist, Kamal Sahib insisted on a night shoot to make the sequence realistic.

It was realistic. The film did badly, but time has been kind to the melody. As it was to Kaif Bhopali's delicate lyrics, which has the listener in a trance as Lata almost whispers the line – 'Jaane Kiske Baahon Se', a reminder that Lata loved to sing the *vilambit* (slow) khayal, a genre she never considered taking up professionally. This poetic stanza was unfortunately truncated in the album, as the emphasis was more on the number of songs.

Talking of poetry, the third Khayyam-Lata song in the collection was mostly around that. A few couplets of the same were as quoted next,

'Bahut aarzoo thi gali ki teri,
So yaan se lahu mein naha kar chale.
Dikhai diye yun ke bekhud kiya,
Hamen aap se bhi juda kar chale'.

Khayyam wove his tune around these couplets in a tribute to poetry from a bygone era. His association with top-notch poets had always resulted in unforgettable melodies. 'Dikhai Diye Yun' is no exception; however, it did add another dimension to his repertoire. Poet Mir Taqi Mir, a poet who preceded Mirza Ghalib by almost seventy-five years, was immortalized in the voice of Lata Mangeshkar some 170 years after he was no more.

Incidentally, this was Khayyam sans his trademark Pahadi.

However, to tag Pahadi as the limit of Khayyam's creativity would be criminal. Tranquil is more likely the correct term. His arrangement for one was characteristically uncluttered. The separation of frequencies in his songs was smooth, a trait that he developed as monetary limitations did not allow him the luxury of a big orchestra during his days of struggle, the 1950s through to early 1970s.

Bazaar (1982), too, was a low-budget film. But Khayyam was big by that time. The orchestra was richer. Arranged by Anil Mohile and recorded at Mehboob Studios, the number of violinists was surely more than what the composer had been using in his pre-1975 period. In the use of the bongo, the conga, the guitar and the mandolin, the composer also presents a degree of modernity in the arrangement.

However, Khayyam avoided the big sound even when he created the magnificence of the evening in 'Dikhai Diye Yun'. The use of the uncharacteristic 'Ga' as the first note in a *mukhda* that predominantly used the notes of raag Yaman imparted to the song a mellow feel. There is a tendency to gravitate towards 'Pa', which also nullifies the stress on Teeva Ma (F sharp), the representative note of Yaman. Nevertheless, the song has a certain masculinity to it; the inflexion 'Ki Bekhud Kiya' sounds fit to be sung by a gruff voice. It is to Lata's credit and immense talent that she negotiated the phrase with her characteristic poignance, unveiling and intensifying the virginal quality of Shabnam (Supriya Pathak).

As did Khayyam and Mohile. Using the violin ensemble in a near-symphonic manner, they captured the emotions floating. The song sequence, set on the terrace of a house in Hyderabad, finds the roving camera focussing on the subtle interplay between the characters as Shabnam welcomes the guests with her song. Salim loves Najma, but she is sleeping with Akhtar; Nasreen loves Sarju but makes way for Shabnam. Shakir Ali Khan (the buyer), Najma (the facilitator), Akhtar (the beneficiary) and Salim (the angry, bearded poet) – all bound to each other in an unholy nexus, each hoping to extract his pound of flesh. The only exception is the guileless Shabnam. She is the one on display in the showroom to be bought by Shakir for INR 5,000, under the garb of convenience called 'marriage'. The fatalistic ending, hovering like a premonition in this supposedly innocuous party scene, is perhaps the reason Khayyam used high notes in the last stanza – 'Bahut aarzoo thi gali ki teri/So yaan se lahu mein naha kar chale'. Mir's poetry in the two lines expresses the sense of loss, of helplessness and of the shattering of dreams.

Mir would have had no way of knowing that his couplet would be one of the fundamental elements in director Sagar Sarhadi's cinema based on a real-life story of a bride sale in Hyderabad.

In stark contrast to the trend of having one or two dedicated lyricists for a film, the song selection for *Bazaar* was done from available poetry. Nawaz, whose poem 'Karoge Yaad Toh' was one of the five to make it in the film, talked to author V. Balaji[4] –

> Mir Taqi Mir had this unique quality of presenting a profound thought as a common day-to-day experience of life. His simplicity connected his poetry with the commoners. The reason 'Dikhai Diye Yun' made it to the final cut in the film.

Something which Lata surely did not mind. And as time would tell, the song grew on her strongly enough to make it to the final cut of her favourites as well.

Rajesh Roshan – relaxed gait

Song

- 'Pal Bhar Mein Yeh Kya Ho Gaya' (*Swami*, 1977)
    - Lyrics: Amit Khanna

Rains, or songs connected with rains, have been a popular attraction in Hindi cinema. During the 1970s, Basu Chatterji (1927–2020), who heralded the middle-of-the-road cinema with his simple tales about simpler people, also brought in rain as the backdrop for a romantic relationship. He found no fixed reason to shoot the rains. Any occasion was welcome. As were the rain shots in his first adaptation of a story by Sarat Chandra Chatterjee (1876–1938). *Swami* (1977). Shabana Azmi, who played the protagonist Mini, mentions:

During *Swami*, the monsoon scenes were shot during the monsoon as well. This was quite remarkable, and you need to give a huge thumbs-up to KK Mahajan (1944–2007) (cinematographer) as he did it without any additional lighting. Particularly during the song 'Pal Bhar Mein Yeh Kya Ho Gaya'.[5]

Rajesh Roshan remains one of the many music directors whose association with Lata Mangeshkar started strongly from his very first film – *Kunwara Baap* (1974), gaining from strength to strength with subsequent films like *Julie* (1975) and *Udhar ka Sindoor* (1976). *Swami* had a solitary Lata song. Used in the background, it was meant to take the narrative forward through the visuals and the relaxed deportment the song exuded. A deportment that defined the world of Mini, the central character, through the camera of KK Mahajan. And the lyrics of Amit Khanna supported by long notes, a comfortable gait and, among others, a string ensemble connecting the antara with the mukhra.

Contrary to the gaiety one associates with rain songs, there is a lot of stillness and silence. 'Pal Bhar Mein Yeh Kya Ho Gaya' does not take place during the rain following a thunderstorm. It happens in a back-to-back manner after the rain has accentuated Mini's romantic spirit. And sealed with a kiss by

Naren (Vikram, playing the lover). The focus of the song is from the point of view of a girl who is lost deeply in love.

The starting notes of this melody were inspired by the opening bars of Olivia Newton John's *Sam* (1974). From there, the tune took a diversion, though the scale remains faithful to the original. Major scales, if not always, were normally used for songs of hope. Rajesh Roshan also uses a flat sixth in the antara, creating a detour from the upscale mood. Of most interest is Lata Mangeshkar's voice modulation. She sounds almost like Shabana Azmi, as Mahajan's roving camera catches the romantic world of Mini – from her dreamy solitude to her kohl-laden eyes meeting those of Naren, the man she was in love with. The song is about Mini sifting through precious moments frozen in time, capturing her vulnerable side. Rajesh Roshan, in an interview with Bhattacharjee, says,[6]

> 'Pal Bhar Mein Yeh Kya Ho Gaya' is one of the finest rendered songs by Lataji for me. Interestingly, we hardly spoke to each other during the recording. That she had grasped the song to a T is obvious. I never did get a chance to rehearse with her. She used to come to the set, learn the song and then render it there and then. Genius! She and Kishore-da (Kumar) became working partners with me. The three of us had a perfect silent understanding! Every time we recorded, it turned into magic. For this song, there were stalwart musicians like Hariprasad-ji (Chaurasia) on the flute, Shiv Kumar-ji (Sharma) on the santoor, and Charanjeet-ji (Singh) (1940–2015) on bass guitar. All the stalwarts worked with me off and on.

Ghulam Mohammed – pure heart

Song

- 'Thade rahiyo o Banke yaar re' (Pakeezah, 1972)
  - Lyrics: Majrooh Sultanpuri

The mujra as a dance form was performed by tawaifs (courtesans) at the mansions of the wealthy or in public places known as kothas. It used to be a combination of the kathak dance, the thumri (a form of Hindustani Classical music) and the occasional ghazal (love song) – and hence, the performers were looked at with a modicum of respect. One can wonder why these tawaifs should be denied the social respect that, say, any other stage performer gets. Both categories of artistes perform for money. In films like Satyajit Ray's (1921–1992) *Jalsaghar* (1958), one observes a lot of respect being paid to the performers. Somewhere down the line, mujra performances became a facade for prostitution. The other reason for the discrimination is probably that one is a tawaif rarely by choice. It is implied that these girls did not have access to formal education or any other vocational skills. Often the dancing skills are handed down from mother to daughter.[7]

Anyone who has followed Lata Mangeshkar's career will vouch for the fact that she was extremely reluctant to sing songs which bordered on any inkling of sex. Cabarets were out; there are very few cabarets which Lata recorded in her lengthy career. Songs involving dance were fine if they were bereft of innuendoes. So, while the vamps have been mostly unlucky not to have Lata as their playback for cabarets, the heroines had rather a hefty share of ad-libbing dance songs by Lata. Even when the song was a mujra.

One such film was *Pakeezah* (aka Pure heart, 1972).

The making of *Pakeezah* is one of the most articulated stories in Indian cine history. Officially launched in 1956 as *Pakeeza*, by the time it was released as *Pakeezah* some sixteen years later, two of the key crew members had passed away: Joseph Wirsching (1903–67), the DoP and Ghulam Mohammed, the music director. Kamal Amrohi, the director of the film, who was also married to Meena Kumari, who played the 'pure heart', initially had set his mind on employing the services of C. Ramchandra for the music. This was just after the mega success of the music of Filmistan's *Anarkali* , until the music of *Mizra Ghalib* (1954) made him shift to Mohammed.

Born in Naal, a village near Bikaner, Rajasthan, India, Mohammed learnt classical music from his father, Nabi Baksh, who was an accomplished tabla (a very popular Indian rhythm instrument) player. It is little wonder that Mohammed became an expert on rhythm instruments, and gradually he picked up forms of Rajasthani folk music as well. He was also trained in dance and would accompany troupes of travelling theatres as an orchestra artiste and a dancer.

Debuting in cinema as tabla player for *Bhatruhari* (1932), Mohammed's main claim to fame was assisting music director Naushad, someone he had introduced to the film world. Considered by experts and aficionados as one who never got his due, God was smiling somewhere. *Pakeezah,* released almost four years after his death, immortalized him.

Lata Mangeshkar's choice of song – 'Thade Rahiyo' – was also, in many ways, a heartfelt tribute to Mohammed. To start with, it was based on a popular Rajasthani raag, Mand. The lyrics by Majrooh Sultanpuri also had the usage of Rajasthani words. 'Thade Rahiyo', the first line of the asthayi of the song, is itself a Rajasthani term that means 'Keep waiting'. While the song was about a nautch girl of Lucknow, it had Rajasthan written all over. The *sargam* (a short musical phrase) used by Lata after the first antara comprises mostly 'tabla-bols', and one could safely infer that Ghulam Mohammed wrote them himself. The change of rhythm from 3/4 to 4/4 and back to 3/4, all within the song, also signifies Mohammed's expertise at navigating through multiple beat patterns within a single melodic structure, something that is not often used in Indian music. Among the instruments, apart from the jhalas on the sitar, prominent are Hazara Singh's slide guitar and Pandit Ram Narayan's sarangi.

While on the subject, it needs to be mentioned that while Mohammed had his musicians and Lata Mangeshkar rehearse the song multiple times, by the time of the recording, he was extremely ill and not in a position to attend the session and solicited the help of Naushad to carry out the recording. However, defying all medical equations, Mohammed came to the studio, sat on a chair and supervised the proceedings.[8]

Notes

1 WhatsApp exchange with Jayanta Gupta, son of Hemen Gupta, on 16 July 2023.

2 Telephonic Interview with Madhuchhanda Chakrabarty on 9 March 2022.

3 Madhuchhanda mentioned the singer's name; however, she requested that the name not be mentioned.

4 Telephonic Interview with Bashar Nawaz by V Balaji in 2012.

5 Telephonic Interview with Shabana Azmi on 10 July 2021.

6 Email correspondence with Rajesh Roshan on 11 October 2021.

7 Anirudha Bhattacharjee and Balaji Vittal, *Gaata Rahe Mera Dil* (Noida: Harper Collins India, 2015).

8 Nalin Shah, *The Man who Made Pakeezah Memorable – Ghulam Mohammed, The Unsung Melodist,* by Raaj Kumar Bothra and Ranjan Sain (Chennai: Notion Press, 2022).

9 The less spoken

Hindi cine music can be a cruel business. Only a few make it to the top; the rest, literally thousands, wither away. Among multiple factors, providence and the inability to create the perception of greatness is one. Composers like Chitragupta and S. Mohinder fall into this category, who, despite their talent, have never been talked about in the same breath as a Naushad, Shankar Jaikishan, a RD or even a Jaidev. Thankfully, Lata remembered their contribution to her career as well, as we have a few songs that create an intense sense of nostalgia.

Chitragupta – the gentle soul

Songs

- 'Dagabaaz ho banke piya' (*Burmah Road*, 1962)
    - Lyrics: Majrooh Sultanpuri
    - Co-singer: Usha Mangeshkar
- 'Dil ka diya jala kar gaya' (*Aakash Deep*, 1965)
    - Lyrics: Majrooh Sultanpuri

Starting his musical journey as a chorus singer and turning into a composer after a short stint as an assistant to S. N. Tripathi (1913–88), Chitragupta is unfortunately someone who could never corner the influence reserved for the Naushads, the Burmans or the Madan Mohans. This is unfortunate, as some of his works are seminal and at par with the best. A career that flourished under a Madras-based banner, AVM, found little or no fillip in Bombay, where he found assignments that were at best categorized as low budget or, to use a Bombay film jargon, B-grade. Despite the handicap of limited resources, monetary or otherwise, he did come up with a few brilliant songs, especially if the singer was Lata Mangeshkar.

And Lata was magnanimous in her appreciation of the same. She was close to the family too and would come down and spend time with Chitragupta's wife in the kitchen, often cooking her favourite dishes and serving them to the children. And Chitragupta ensured that a generation who loved viewing low-budget films in dusty cinema halls was brought up on a healthy diet of Lata Mangeshkar's songs. After all, who would remember nondescript films like *Barkha* (1957), *Guest House* (1959), *Madame XYZ* (1959), *Chand Mere Aja* (1960), *Patang* (1960) or *Bezubaan* (1962)? The authors had a quick-fire discussion on the same and inferred that the Lata-Chitragupta combo was as good as any other combo in their prime. Just that the films were bad enough to spur any recall.

Consequently, Lata might have faced a huge challenge in selecting her songs of Chitragupta for the album. Her final choices – two of them – perhaps reflect a basic rule: what sounds good to the public is good material. One might note that she chose two songs and not one, in contrast to her solitary selections for much more famous music directors like C. Ramchandra or Hemant Kumar. A probable reason could be that *My Favourites Volume 1* did not have a single song from Chitragupta's stable. And she wanted to make amends.

'Dagabaaz ho banke piya', the first song, was from a film as inconspicuous as the ones mentioned in the write up. Who, in their senses, would remember a film named *Burmah Road*? Even hardcore 1960s fans do not. Forget the film if you want to, but the song would keep you captivated. A dance number that was handled with subtlety, and we can find traces of the Shankar Jaikishan school.

That was the beauty of Chitragupta's compositions. He patented a form that was not aligned to a particular framework. Given the requirement, he would model himself on a pattern representative of more famous composers.

Another reason why Lata went for this song could be that she had to include a duet with her sister, Usha Mangeshkar. Since starting her singing career as a teenager, Usha has remained Lata's most faithful follower, fan and co-singer. Most programmes of Lata would feature Usha singing duets with her sister, apart from singing the one-off solo. Despite being a Mangeshkar, Usha never had a strong career. The duets with Lata helped her share the limelight with her more illustrious elder sister. Per Lata, her favourites include 'Tumko piya dil diya' (Shikari, 1963) and the song she chose for the album, 'Dagabaaz ho banke piya'. 'Tumko piya dil diya', composed by G. S. Kohli, has been a favourite of HMV. 'Dagabaaz'... probably needed more traction, and Lata ensured it happened via her own favourites.

While casting aspersions on the selection of the first song, there can be no ambiguity regarding the second one though. 'Dil ka diya' was a certified hit. Sung in almost a whispering cadence and supplemented with the tinkle of temple bells, it is one of Lata's most loved songs of the 1960s. As in the previous song, this too was a mix of styles, and in this case, one can identify the feel of multiple raags, namely Pahadi, Jhinjhoti, Jaijaiwanti and Janasammohini. It was picturized aesthetically, with Vani, the mute heroine (played by Nimmi), moving her lips with the song, which is played on a turntable. In the 1960s, Chitragupta had the good fortune of working with director Phani Majumdar, who, after a long stint in Singapore in the 1950s, was back to Bombay and made films that had the buy-in of the educated class. He gave his cast and crew a lot of freedom, and this worked in favour of Chitragupta, who created some lovely music in his films.

A bachelor of arts in economics followed by a master's in journalism, Chitragupta was a representative of the educated lot, during a time when musicians in Bombay, barring a few like SD or Salil Chowdhury, had hardly cleared the hurdle of high school examination. Working for Phani Majumdar, whose erudition was acknowledged by the film folk, helped. *Aakash Deep*, written and made by Majumdar, was about the clash of the proletariat and the bourgeois. While it has not aged well, it received moderately complimentary reviews when released, with at least two songs being lauded as classics today, the other being 'Mujhe dard-e-dil ka pata na tha', sung by Md. Rafi.

While on the Phani Majumdar-Chitragupta track, we wonder why Lata chose to give her duet with Mahendra Kapoor – 'Aaja re mere pyar ke rahi' – from *Oonche Log* (1966), another Phani Majumdar film, a miss. This Kalavati-based melody has a strong haunting quotient, amplified by the reverb and the mysterious manner in which the heroine K. R. Vijaya's face is fleetingly shown, that goes hand in glove with the dark subject.

From dark alleys and communist lanes, our book moves to a song set in the parched and bone-dry desert of the Caucasus region, where two lovers met only to die.

S. Mohinder – solitary reaper

Song

- 'Guzra hua zamana aata naheen dobara' (*Shirin Farhad*, 1956)
    - Lyrics: Tanvir Naqvi

India International School is an ethnic institution founded in 1982 in Virginia by Non-Resident Indians. The music department was started by someone who had migrated to the United States after a not-so-successful career in the Hindi film music industry. S Mohinder.[1] After teaching there for a week, he left, having generally retired from active musical life. Twenty-five years later, he received an invitation from the institution to preside over as the chief guest during the school's silver jubilee function. This was something he could not refuse, and he was also happy to find a few students singing songs that he had composed in Bombay. After some time, he was requested to come on stage, which he did. And as expected, he was asked to sing 'Guzra hua zamana', his composition from the 1956 film *Shirin Farhad*. He started singing. By the time he was into the repeat of the refrain, many in the audience had started singing with him in unison.

Mohinder stopped. The audience kept on singing and sang the antaras, three in total.[2]

This, briefly, is proof enough for a song's everlasting popularity. A fifty-year-old song from a film that most have never seen was being sung by almost everyone in an auditorium. Lata Mangeshkar would go on record, mentioning that this song would be included in almost every second collection of hers published by HMV.[3]

Technically, there is nothing special about the song. It is in raag Yamini Bilawal, and the rhythm pattern is 4/4, combos often used in Hindi film music from the 1940s through the late 1960s. And that is exactly why it is so difficult for a song, having credentials that match a few hundreds, to be a regular in compilations.

The reason lies in the song's simplicity. And hummable quotient. While Mohinder's songs can hardly be labelled as simple, as he would often introduce *murkis* and *harkats* that are beyond untrained singers, he would keep the tune simple and negotiable. Plus, 'Guzra hua zamana' had very soulful lyrics that fitted the tune well. In this context, it needs to be mentioned that S. Mohinder would compose to lyrics and not vice versa.

The lyricist in this case was Tanvir Naqvi. And this brings us to the history behind the making of the song. Naqvi, who was famous in pre-partition India for his songs like 'Awaaz de kahan hai' and 'Jawan Hai Mohobaat' (both from the 1946 film *Anmol Ghadi*), had migrated to Pakistan and settled down with his two wives, one of whom was Noor Jehan's elder sister. He had come down to India at the behest of K. Asif (1922–71) who was making *Mughal-e-Azam* (1960). The proposal did not fructify, as Naushad, the composer of the film, was already working with Shakeel Badayuni. However, Naqvi had a long-term visa, and S. Mohinder suggested that it be put to effective use and offered him to write lyrics for *Shirin Farhad* where he was working. 'Guzra hua zamana' was the first song Naqvi wrote for S. Mohinder.[4] One assumes the film was delayed, as by the time the film was released, there were a few more films in which Naqvi and S. Mohinder had collaborated, including the Madhubala productions' *Naata* (1955).

During that time, Madhubala had placed a clause in her contracts that mandated Lata Mangeshkar as her playback. And incidentally, Lata Mangeshkar and S. Mohinder were not on talking terms when *Shirin Farhad* and *Naata* were in production. Lata would, at that time, visit Naqvi's house on Sundays to meet Eidan, his wife, as she was Noor Jehan's sister and a good friend. Eidan invited Mohinder one Sunday afternoon, when Lata was also there. He was asked to sing his latest composition, 'Dekhte dekhte jal gaya aasmaan' (*Naata*, 1955), which Lata loved and agreed to sing, and the impasse was resolved.[5]

And then we had 'Guzra Hua Zamana'. Undoubtedly a brilliant song, but unfortunately, it remains the Mohinder-Lata combo's only claim to fame in Hindi cine music today.

Notes

1 Email exchange with Dhananjaya Kumar of India International School on 25 December 2023.

2 Guftagoo with S. Mohinder on Sansad TV https://www.youtube.com/watch?v=44-9cl-fQDc.

3 Yatindra Mishra, *Lata Sur Gatha* (New Delhi: Vani Prakashan, 2016).

4 Surmayi Baatein with S. Mohinder by Falguni Upadhyay https://www.youtube.com/watch?v=T1yy6FbdZX8.

5 Ibid. S. Mohinder further mentions that Lata was not happy with him as he was using her sister Asha Bhosle's vocals more for his compositions.

10 The lesser heard

While the songs Lata chose for the album were majorly from her work for the cinema, there were a few non-film songs as well. The following section discusses the same. Only one song – out of the five – in this chapter is from a film.

Talking about non-film music, Lata had always been a strong votary of devotional songs. Her first six non-film songs, recorded in 1948, were for a ballet about Gautam Buddha. The number of Meera bhajans – songs written by Meerabai, the sixteenth-century Hindu mystic and poet who was also the queen of Mewar in Rajasthan, India – sung by her, including songs used for the cinema, is thirty-eight. And these are by far the most well-known among the 257 non-film Hindi songs she recorded in her lifetime.

Lata also sang a few ghazals. These did not attain the popularity expected of a Lata Mangeshkar song, though musically they are among the best of her repertoire. Generically, non-film songs, apart from a strong ghazal and bhajan wave in the early to mid-1980s, remained commercially unviable. In the absence of a visual angle, their popularity was mostly confined to the living room of the ultra-rich with a pretence of intellectualism. Or the literati who refused to espouse pop culture as part of their own. However, like all magnificent works of art, these songs have had a reasonably good shelf life.

Hridaynath Mangeshkar – family

Songs

- 'Thane kain kain bol sanava' (non-film, 1968)
    - Lyrics: Meerabai
- 'Ghiri ghiri ghatayen aasmaan par' (non-film, 1969)
    - Lyrics: Sumitra Kumari Sinha (name printed: Sumitra Lahiri)
- 'Tum aasha vishwas hamare' (*Subah*, 1982)
    - Lyrics: Pandit Narendra Sharma

Hridaynath is Lata Mangeshkar's youngest sibling and only brother, who was all of four-and-a-half years old when his father Deenanath Mangeshkar (1900–42), the doyen of Marathi classical and stage musicals (*natyageet*), passed away young.

His future in music was assured and inescapable, along with the pampering and influence of four loving sisters. While still in his teens, he received some training in classical music from the legendary Ustad Amir Khan (1912–74) (himself a pupil of Ustad Aman Ali Khan, who formally taught Lata Mangeshkar), but Hridaynath maintains that 'Didi' Lata remains his foremost guru. Before venturing into composing, the young Hridaynath was already singing by the age of fifteen, notably a song 'Ye duniya kaisi hai bhagwan' for Naushad in the film *Diwana* in 1952 (Asha Bhosle proudly claims that his unbroken voice comes closer to hers than any of the other sisters).

Once he became a composer, he carved a niche for himself as one who championed the cause of Marathi literature, showcasing the talents of well (and less) known poets such as Shanta Shelke (1922–2002), Suresh Bhat (1932–2003), Vasant Bapat (1922–2002), Namdeo Mahanor (1942–2023) and Balkavi (Trimbak Bapuji Thombre) (1889 or 1890–1918), as well as legends who were deservedly paid tribute in full albums: Meera (two albums, in fact), Ghalib and the Maharashtrian saint Gyaneshwar. Using a maverick approach in fashioning unpredictable tunes (he acknowledges Salil Chowdhury as an inspiration), his work remains unsurpassed in popularity among Marathi listeners.

Exceptional among these already complex tunes are the songs he composed for Lata Mangeshkar. *Lata Mangeshkar Sings Ghalib*, recorded in 1969 and *Chala vahi des*, the second LP of Meera Bhajans, recorded in 1974, was both family affairs, with Usha Mangeshkar doing the painting for the album covers.

The first song Lata chose from the 261 songs that her brother composed for her is 'Thane kain kain bol'. Originally released on the first *Meera* album in 1968, the lyrics are attributed to the eponymous legendary Rajput princess and devotee of Lord Krishna. The Lord is in his romantic and playful '*Ras Leela*' form here (the Krishna from the epic 'Mahabharata' is a different persona altogether), and the song speaks of her love for him amidst a background of '*Gopis*' dancing the dandiya. Although very light-hearted compared to her other songs on this album, all have been recorded in her unembellished voice, with bare instrumentation and not a trace of added echo or reverb effects.

'Ghiri ghiri ghatayen', the next Hridaynath composition in the list, is a rare and unexpected inclusion, as the song was almost out of circulation in the 1980s. A non-film song whose lyrics have been incorrectly credited to Sumitra Lahiri in this compilation, it tells of rain, a literally perennial and ever-popular motif in the Indian romantic song. GCI/EMI has bungled big time on this; the song was originally published under their Regal label in 1969 as part of an LP named *Varsha Ritu* (songs of the rainy season), and the name of the lyricist on the album cover (and the record) was Sumitra Kumari Sinha, a famous poet and author. Sumitra Lahiri, who became the lyricist on the rebound due to a misprint, was primarily a singer of ghazals who also sang and composed for the cinema. She never wrote poetry that was put to tune and recorded by Lata Mangeshkar.

Appropriately set in raag Malhar, and with a santoor's staccato notes standing in for the patter of raindrops, Lata Mangeshkar makes the complex *taans* look effortlessly easy. Her voice creates the impression of bobbing about on a thin layer of water. It is unfortunate that despite Lata promoting this song, it has remained a lesser-heard and unappreciated gem.

Now for the third selection, a rather predictable one at that. One of the poets who Lata had always considered a father figure is Pandit Narendra Sharma. Hence, it was surprising that his chance came quite late in the album. But better late than never, as the saying goes, and Lata makes amends by selecting 'Tum aasha vishwas hamare', a devotional song from the film *Subah* (1982). It is a prayer sung outdoors in a woman's reformatory, reminiscent of 'Gagana sadana' from *Umbartha* (1982), the Marathi version of *Subah*. The album for the film was released by Music India Limited, and this was, most probably, used as part of *My Favourites* with permission from the parent company.

The song is an invocation to an all-powerful almighty and was extremely popular in its time, so much so that 'Tumi pathor chokheo je drishti', a Bengali version, was recorded in 1983 to the lyrics of Gouri Prasanna Majumdar.

Fayyaz Shaukat and K. Mahavir – lesser knowns

Songs

- Har ik baat pe (non-film, 1961)
  - Composer: Fayyaz Ahmed Khan (name printed: Faiyaaz Shaukat)
  - Lyrics: Mirza Ghalib
- Sanjh bari ghar aaja re piya (non-film, 1973)
  - Composer: K. Mahavir
  - Lyrics: Abhilash

Ustad Fayyaz Ahmed Khan was a grand-nephew of Khansaheb Abdul Karim Khan (1872–1937), the founder of Kirana Gharana. A multi-faceted personality, he was a singer of Hindustani classical music, a poet writing under the nom de plume of Fayyaz Jaipuri, a music guru to many, including Meera Dev Burman (wife of SD and mother of RD),[1] and a composer known for his innovations, one of which included raag Chandraprabha.

In 1961, he composed two ghazals of Mirza Ghalib for Lata Mangeshkar, of which *Har ik baat pe*, tuned in Yaman, was included in this collection. The name of the composer inscribed on the Columbia record was Faiyyaz-Shaukat, which, in *My Favourites Volume 2*, became Faiyyaz Shaukat, with the hyphen missing. While Ustad Fayyaz Ahmed Khan worked with Talat Mahmood, Jagjit Singh and Sulakshana Pandit, among others, the name Faiyyaz Shaukat never got repeated, leading to speculations about the identity of the composer. Dr Ravindra Shrikhande of Ratnagiri, India, wrote to Hridaynath Mangeshkar, who, two days after Lata was hospitalized in early January 2022, replied that the composers were Ustad Fayyaz Ahmed Khan and his brother Niyaz Ahmed Khan (1924–2003).[2] However, why Niyaz Ahmed Khan would assume the pseudonym Shaukat remained a mystery.

Sarfaraz, Fayyaz Ahmed Khan's son, in a telephonic interview with Bhattacharjee, cleared the mix-up. 'You see, Shaukat bhai was a very good friend of my father. He had accompanied my father to the recording, and put in his name, saying – *Mera naam bhi ho jayega* (My name will also become famous). The song was created in one day.'[3]

And Lata learnt, rehearsed and recorded the song in a day too. Despite the attention to detail mandated for a song that was in Urdu, she had prepared herself well. Her Urdu diction, courtesy of her tutelage under Maulana Mehboob Ali, remained flawless. Her command over sur was never in doubt. Add to that, she modulated her voice to create a coarseness factor mandatory for ghazals sung in the subcontinent. The song also served as a tribute to the composer, who, like William Shakespeare, Ingrid Bergman and Bidhan Chandra Roy, was one of the very few to die on his birthday, 11 May 1987, a year before the album was released.

* * *

Jaipur, the capital of Rajasthan, is one of the oldest gharanas of kathak dance in India. Music and kathak being related art forms, P. Mahadev Prasad Raggi (birth and death years not available publicly), a student of the gharana, was a big name in Punjabi devotional music, being one of the organizers of the *Harballabh Sangeet Sammelan*. He was close to Masterji Khemchand Prakash, and his eldest son, K. Madan Prakash also assisted Masterji for some time. The third son, Kathak Mahavir, became a music trainer and composer in Bombay. Among his students, we have present-day musicians Bombay Jayashri and Devaki Pandit.[4]

One of his students was Arun Date (1934–2018), a popular singer in Marathi. Date helped in taking some of Mahavir's semiclassical compositions to Hridaynath Mangeshkar, who liked them, and subsequently Lata Mangeshkar was approached with the idea of a four-song album. Lata Mangeshkar loved the compositions, and an EP named *Geet-Ghazal* (number 7EPE 4016) was released in 1973.[5] By that time, Usha Mangeshkar had already sung two songs under Mahavir.

The first track from the four that Lata okayed was 'Aankh se aankh milata hai koi'. That was used in *My Favourites Volume 1*. For *Volume 2*, Lata chose a stunning composition in raag Marwa, 'Saanjh bhayi ghar aaja re piya'. The inclusion of the song became a dedication, as K. Mahavir had passed away on 27 November 1987.

It is unfortunate that, despite his immense talent and devotion to music, Mahavir could never make it to the big league. There were instances where he would have to sell his compositions to established music directors of the film industry.[6] Thankfully, Lata Mangeshkar ensured that he is remembered by, at least, a section of music lovers. All four songs she had sung for him were re-released in 1993 on a CD named *Non-Film Treasures* (number CD PMLP 5727). This included 'Ghiri Ghatayen' and her songs for Fayyad Ahmed Khan as well.

Notes

1. Telephonic conversation with Sarfaraz Ahmed Khan, son of Ustad Fayyaz Ahmed Khan, on 19 February 2024.
2. Telephonic conversation with Dr Ravindra Shrikhande on 19 February 2024.
3. Op Cit, Khan.
4. Telephonic conversation with Mahavir's son Rajeev K. Mahavir on 21 February 2024 and with Sabesh Subramanium, brother of Bombay Jayashri, on 22 February 2024.
5. Ibid.
6. Ibid.

11 The last song

Ravindra Jain – Raj Kapoor's last magnum opus

Song

- 'Husn pahadon ka' (*Ram Teri Ganga Maili*, 1985)
  - Lyrics: Ravindra Jain
  - Co-singer: Suresh Wadkar (born 1955)

The songs you just heard have many memories and stories from my life. In this melodious journey, the form of lyrics, musical phrases and orchestra kept changing. And whatever is there now will also change. Yes, one thing has not changed or diminished, that is your love. I am thankful to all of you for this which is increasing day by day. I wish you all the best. Namaskar.

Well, this is how Lata summed up her selections in this album. Music for the performing artiste is like experiences that live on their own. An abstract kind of memory. Personal. Yet, universal.

Curiously, she did not mention someone special. RK. While not connected to music directly, Raj, in her words, was the brains behind all the music in his films. For Raj, Lata was one of the strongest inspirations in his life, part of the coterie of women whom he termed as 'The woman in white'. Hence, it is even more intriguing to find that none of the Shankar

Jaikishan songs in *Volume 2* – RK's in-house composers – are from films by Raj.

Perhaps to seal any debate that could arise as a result, Lata, just like she had done in *Volume 1*, chose a song from *Ram Teri Ganga Maili* (*RTGM*) as the last song of the album. While the film has received mixed reviews for its focus on nudity, people were unanimous in their appreciation of the music. The album remains one of the best of the otherwise dreaded 1980s decade. Ravindra Jain, known to work with singer Hemlata in smaller films, touched gold. The only composer in Hindi cinema who would write most of his lyrics, he would often ask the singer to read the script to him because of his visual impairment. One assumes that RK had described the shot divisions to him in quite some detail, as his music augmented the visual glamour of the Himalayas, one of the attractions of the film. Unfortunately, *RTGM* remained the only film he would do for Raj. It was Lata's last for Raj as well, as *RTGM* would be the last film he directed. *Heena* (1991), a film that was in his mind for a long time but started after *RTGM*, was completed after his death by his son Randhir Kapoor, and Jain's music was again labelled as superlative.

12 Summing up

The public perception is that Lata Mangeshkar's best work happened pre-1975. Lata's selection in *Volume 2* has forty-five out of the fifty songs, a whopping 95 per cent, from the period 1948–73. For a collection that was published in 1988, when Lata Mangeshkar was basking in the limelight of four decades of national admiration and still churning out hits, it showed a lot of restraint and character in not being influenced by the recency factor.

One can also attribute this to a psychological pattern. You connect more with your days of struggle and less when it comes to a stage of 'Business as usual'.

However, any compilation comes with its own set of controversies. When one finds that two composers, S-J and Roshan, out of the twenty-seven chosen ones (7 per cent) contribute 20 per cent of the songs, there is bound to be disagreements. Especially with C. Ramchandra soliciting only one mention. The complete absence of Ravi (1926–2012) and the duo of Kalyanji Anandji is startling, more so because they were missing in *Volume 1* as well. Both had some outstanding compositions for her. Had Lata been aware that her selection would lead to a historical reassessment of her work, she might have exercised caution and chosen, maybe, one song per composer.

Or she might not have.

One assumes that the inner Lata Mangeshkar will remain an enigma. By not choosing a few obvious ones, she probably let her silence speak. Whether it spoke of abstraction or guile is subject to the listener's reaction to the chosen ones. Forthcoming and ongoing debates, especially on a few favourites being given a miss, probably are part of the package.

Having said that, the momentous success of *Volume 2* prompted GCI to release a four-cassette collection the following year to celebrate sixty years of Lata Mangeshkar. Titled 'Lata Mangeshkar – Diamonds Forever (60 Years, 60 Songs)', it broke all existing sales records.

Acknowledgements

The authors like to put on record the names, in alphabetical order, of the following friends, scribes and lovers of music in general who helped in adding value to the book.

Aloka Nanjappa, Archisman Mozumder, Arunkumar Deshmukh, Balaji Vittal, Bhaskar Datta, Deepa Buty, Indrajit Banerjee, Falguni Upadhyay, Jayanta Gupta, Kanhaya Lal Pandey, Dr Mandar Bichu, Murtaza Partapurwala, Pavan Jha, Ranjan Biswas, Dr Ravindra Shrikhande, Sabesh Subramaniam, (Late) Sharad Dutt, Snehasis Chatterjee, Sudheer Kulkarnee, Prof Doc (PhD) Surjit Singh, Shivani Zaveri and Yasir Abassi.

We were also fortunate to interview a few film-related personalities at various times in our lives, and some of their inputs were used in this book. Again, in alphabetical order, they are:

Asha Bhosle, (Late) Bashar Nawaz, Chhaya Ganguli, (Late) Dattaram Wadkar, Dhananjaya Kumar, Kankan Dasgupta, Ketan Anand, Madhuchhanda Chakrabarty, Moushumi Chatterjee, Pyarelal Sharma, Rajeev K Mahavir, Rajesh Roshan, Sarfaraz Ahmed Khan, Shabana Azmi, (Late) Shammi Kapoor, and Vikash Desai.

What is a book without a picture? We are thankful to Prachitee Tushar Shetty for the wonderful graphite sketch of Lata Mangehskar, something she did in a record time. To Jai Viraat Singh for providing the audio recordings and the album cover, and to Tapojyoti Sarkar for cleaning the picture to go on the cover.

In retrospect, we have tried to thank all who added value to the book, and apologize if we have missed anyone.

Finally, we thank our editor Natalie Sarrazin for placing faith in us and taking the book from conception to fruition.

Index

Abhilash xxv, 111
Adhikari, Sudarshan 44
Adil, Vishwamitra (Vishwamitter) 35
Ali, Maulana Mehboob 112
Ali, Naushad xxiii, 21, 23–5, 39, 62, 95–6, 99, 104, 108
Aman, Zeenat 74
Ameeta 26
Amrohi, Kamal 88, 95
Anand, Chetan 27, 35, 37, 64, 87
Anand, Dev 5, 27–8, 46, 74–5, 82
Anand, Vijay 35, 71, 85
Anandghan (Lata's *nom de plume* as composer) 1
Asif, K 104
Athaiya, Satyendra xxvi, 7
Azmi, Kaifi xxv, 61, 83, 85–6
Azmi, Shabana 92–3, 97

Badayuni, Shakeel xxvi, 23, 25, 105
Bakshi, Anand 25, 27, 69, 76, 81
Bali, Geeta 40
Balkavi 109
Banu, Saira 20–1
Bapat, Vasant 109
Barabankavi, Khumar 25, 57
Baran, Timir 5
Begum Akhtar 8
Begum, Shamshad 51
Behl, Bunty 87
Bergman, Ingrid 112
Bhagwan 51
Bhandari, Mahipal Chandra 1
Bharatan, Raju 37, 58
Bhat, Suresh 109
Bhattacharya, Ajoy 30
Bhattacharya, Shurjo 82
Bhende, Uma 78
Bhopali, Kaif, xxv 86, 88
Bhosle, Asha xii, xvi, 11, 15–16, 22, 51, 72, 76, 82, 106, 108
Biswas, Anil xxii, 1, 6–9
'Bombay' Jayashri 113–14
Bombay Talkies 3–5, 9, 27
Bose, Bela 78
Bose, Kamal 55

Brynner, Yul 75
Burman, Meera Dev 111
Burman, Rahul Dev xxiii, xxiv, 1, 30, 39, 62, 66, 69–76, 82, 99–100, 111
Burman, Sachin Dev xix, xxiv, 5–6, 23, 26–30, 37, 39, 53, 73, 100, 102, 111

Caesar's Palace Hotel, Bombay 74
Chakrabarty, Madhuchhanda 88, 97
Chandavarkar, Leena 80
Chatterjee, Moushumi 46–7
Chatterjee, Sarat Chandra 92
Chatterji, Basu 91
Chaurasia, Hariprasad 73, 86, 93
Chhaya, Laxmi 18
Chitragupta, *see* Srivastav, Chitragupta
Chowdhury, Salil xxiv, 49, 52–6, 84, 102, 109

Dasgupta, Kankan 55, 59
Date, Arun 113
Dattaram, *see* Wadkar, Dattaram
Davjekar, Datta 1
Desai, Vasant xxiv, 39, 43–4, 46–7
Desai, Vikash 44–5, 47
Devidas, Alexander 29
Dey, Manna xii, 14, 22, 27, 31
Dharmendra 29, 64
Dhawan, Prem xxv, 4
Dubey, Vijay Kishore, xv–xvi
Dutt, Geeta 28, 51, 78
Dutt, Guru 85
Dutt, Sharad xxiv, 47
Dutta, Himangshu 5, 30

Eidan 105

Faiyyaz Shaukat, *see* Khan, Fayyaz Ahmed
Famous Studios 12
Farida 17
Film Center Studio 66
Filmfare (Award) 34, 63–4, 67
Filmfare (magazine) 25
Filmistan xiv, 2–4, 27, 52, 95
Fish Tail Lodge, Pokhara 74

Gandhi, Indira 41
Ganguli, Chhaya 36–7, 114
Ganguly, Ram 12–13
Ganguly, Sachin 27
GCI, *see* Gramophone Company of India, the
Ghalib, Mirza xxv, 89, 109, 111–12

Ghosh, Pannalal 8
Gopi Krishna 45
Gramophone Company of India (GCI), the xiv, xv, xvi, 71, 82, 110, 118
Grant, Cary 75
Guha, Dulal 29, 37
Guha, Putul 29, 37
Gupta, Hemen 85, 97
Gyaneshwar 109

Haider, Ghulam xxii, 1–5, 7–9, 42
Harballabh Sangeet Sammelan 113
Hemant Kumar, *see* Mukherjee, Hemant Kumar
Hemlata 116
His Master's Voice (HMV) xiv, xv, 6, 13, 28, 36, 54, 101, 104
Hitchcock, Alfred 85
HMV, *see* His Master's Voice
Hollywood xi
Husain, Nasir 71
Husain, Tahir 73
Husnlal-Bhagatram xxiii, 39–40
Hussain, Sajjad xxiv, 49, 57–9

Indivar xxv, 31, 33

Jaidev, *see* Verma, Jaidev
Jaikishan, *see* Shankar-Jaikishan
Jain, Ravindra xxiv, xxvi, 115–16
Jaipuri, Hasrat xxv, 11, 12, 16, 21, 43
Jalalabadi, Qamar xxv, 41, 43
Jayashri Ramnath, *see* 'Bombay' Jayashri

Kalyanji-Anandji 19, 117
Kapoor, Mahendra 51, 102
Kapoor, Raj (RK) 12–13, 15, 31, 41, 115–16
Kapoor, Randhir 116
Kapoor, Rishi 41
Kapoor, Shammi 14, 22
Kardar, A.R. 21
Karim, Abdul 17
Kaushal, Kamini 3, 5, 9
Khan, Aamir 73
Khan, Abdul Karim 111
Khan, Ali Akbar 14, 46
Khan, Allaudin 32
Khan, Aman Ali 31, 108
Khan, Amanath 4
Khan, Amir 108
Khan, Bade Ghulam Ali 29, 66
Khan, Fayyaz Ahmed 10, 22, 111–12, 114
Khan, Mehboob 24
Khan, Niyaz Ahmed 112

Khan, Nusrat Fateh Ali 41
Khan, Rais 66, 86–7
Khan, Raja Mehdi Ali xxvi, 80
Khan, Shah Rukh 24
Khan, Vilayat 66–7
Khanna, Amit xxv, 91–2
Khanna, Rajesh 87
Khayyam xxiii, 83, 86–90
Khosla, Raj 79, 80
Kohli, Madan Mohan xxiii, 19, 43, 59, 61–7, 80, 100
Krishan, Rajendra xxvi, 39, 49
Kumar, Ashok 3, 27, 32
Kumar, Dhananjaya 105
Kumar, Kishore 5, 9, 35, 51, 69, 74–5, 93
Kumar, Pradeep 32
Kumar, Rajendra 18
Kumar, Sanjeev 29
Kumar, Udhav xxvi, 34
Kumar, Uttam 18–19, 22
Kumari, Meena 29, 32, 95
Kumkum 16–17

Lahiri, Sumitra, *see* Sinha, Sumitra Kumari
Laxmikant (Kudalkar), *see* Laxmikant-Pyarelal
Laxmikant-Pyarelal (L-P) xix, xxiii, 15, 17, 24, 63, 69, 76–81
Lord, Kersi 1
Lucknavi, Behzad xxv, 6, 8
Ludhianvi, Sahir xxvi, 31–5
Lyallpuri, Naqsh xxv, 61

Madan Mohan, *see* Kohli, Madan Mohan
Madhubala 21, 25, 105
Mahajan, K.K. 92
Mahanor, Namdeo 109
Mahavir, K. xxiii, 111, 113–14
Mahavir, Rajeev K 114
Mahipal, *see* Bhandari, Mahipal Chandra
Mahmood, Talat 35, 51, 112
Majumdar, Phani 8, 102
Mangeshkar, Deenanath 108
Mangeshkar, Hridaynath xxiii, 77, 108–9, 112–13
Mangeshkar, Usha 70, 77, 81, 99, 101, 109
Manto, Saadat Hasan 4
Master Vinayak 8
Meerabai xxv, 107, 108
Mehboob, *see* Khan, Mehboob
Mehboob Studios 88–9
Mir, Mir Taqi xxv, 86, 89, 91
Mistry, Jal 87
Mohammed, Ghulam xxii, 17, 83, 94–7
Mohile, Anil 89–90
Mohinder, S. xxiv, 99, 103–6

Mukerji, Sasadhar (S. Mukerji) 3, 27
Mukesh 18–19, 31, 33
Mukherjee, Hemant Kumar, aka Hemanta Kumar x, xiv, xxiii, 46–7, 83–5, 100
Mukherjee, Indrani 87
Mukherjee, Sandhya 56
Mumtaz 78

Nabi Baksh 95
Nagrath, Roshan Lal ix, xxiv, 23, 31–4, 117
Nanjappa, Aloka 53–4, 59
Naqvi, Tanvir xxvi, 103–5
Narayan, Ram 96
Nargis 13, 17–18, 33
Naug, Biren 85
Naushad, *see* Ali, Naushad
Navketan 27–8
Nawaz, Bashar 97
Nayyar, O.P., (OP, Opee) 40, 62, 69
Newton-John, Olivia 93
Nimmi 16, 96, 102
Nishi 78
Nivedita 29
Noor Jehan 3–4, 41–3, 51, 104–5

Pancham, *see* Burman, Rahul Dev
Pandey, Kanhaya Lal xxi
Pandey, Rakesh 66
Pandit, Devaki 113
Pandit, Sulakshana 112
Panipati, Nazim xxv, 1, 44
Pathak, Supriya 90
Polydor xv
Prakash, Khemchand xxiii, 1, 4–6, 8, 113
Prakash, Madan K 113
Pran 40
Prasad, Samta 44
Premlata 40
Pyarelal (Sharma), *see* Laxmikant-Pyarelal

Raag
- Abhogi 16
- Asavari 41
- Bageshri 16
- Bhairavi 14
- Bhoopali 20
- Bihag 26
- Chandraprabha 111
- Gara 33
- Gaud Malhar 34
- Jaijaiwanti 102
- Janasammohini 102
- Jhinjhoti 102
- Kalavati 79, 102
- Kalyan 29, 65
- Kedar 65
- Khamaj 19, 70

Maalgunji 46
Madhuvanti 66, 80
Malhar 110
Mand 96
Manjh Khamaj 34, 42
Marwa 113
Nat 5
Pahadi 25, 34, 42, 58, 87–9, 102
Shivranjani 13, 80
Suddha Kalyan 29
Tilak Kaamod 19
Yaman 90, 112
Yaman Kalyan 65
Yamini Bilawal 104
Rafi, Mohammed 15, 23, 25–6, 42, 51, 102
Raggi, Mahadev Prasad 113
Rai, Himansu 9
Rajvansh, Priya 64
Ramani, Sheila 35
Ramchandra, C (Chitalkar) x, xxii, 49–52, 95, 100, 117
Rana, Libi, *see* Nivedita
Ranjit Studios 5
Ravi (Sharma, Ravi Shankar) 117
Ray, Satyajit 94
RD, RDB, R.D. Burman, *see* Burman, Rahul Dev
Reeves, Steve 78
Romancing with Life 75
Roongta 45
Roshan, Hritik 32
Roshan, Ira 33
Roshan, Rajesh xxiv, 83, 91–3, 97
Roshan, Rakesh 32
Roshan, *see* Nagrath, Roshan Lal
Roy, Dr. Bidhan Chandra 112
Royal Albert Hall 15, 42, 64, 71, 82

Sadhana 26, 79
Sahni, Balraj 35
Sahu, Kishore 28
Sajjad, *see* Hussain, Sajjad
Sarhadi, Sagar 91
Sathyu, M.S. 64, 67
SDB, S.D. Burman, *see* Burman, Sachin Dev
Shah, Chandulal 5
Shailendra xxvi, 11–12, 18, 52, 56, 59
Shakespeare, William 112
Shammi 33
Shankar, *see* Shankar-Jaikishan
Shankar-Jaikishan (S-J) xxiv, 11–20, 24, 28, 31, 39, 40, 55–6, 69, 78, 86, 88, 99, 101, 115
Shantaram, V. 44–5
Sharda 15
Sharma, Arun 82

Sharma, Ganesh 77
Sharma, Narendra xxv, 35, 108, 115
Sharma, Pyarelal, *see* Laxmikant-Pyarelal
Sharma, Shiv Kumar 44, 86, 93
Shaukat, Fayyaz, *see* Khan, Fayyaz Ahmed
Shelke, Shanta 109
Shrikhande, Ravindra 112, 114
Shyam Sundar xxiv, 39, 41–3
Shyama 33
Singh, Bhupinder (Bhupendra) 66, 73
Singh, Charanjeet 93
Singh, Dara 78
Singh, Jagjit 112
Sinha, Sumitra Kumari 108
Srivastav, Chitragupta xxii, 99–102
Sukhdev, S. 35
Sultan, Rehana 67
Sultanpuri, Majrooh xxv, 24, 26, 69, 94, 96, 99
Sur Mandir, Bombay 74
Suraiya 40–1, 43, 51
Sureela Bal Kala Kendra 76–7

Tagore, Rabindranath 53, 85
Tripathi, S. N. 99

Upadhyay, Falguni 106

Verma, Jaidev xxiii, 23, 34–6, 99
Vijaya, K. R. 103
Vikram 93
Vyjayantimala 19

Wadkar, Dattaram 12, 21
Wadkar, Suresh 115
Wallah, Hari 32
Watergate Hotel, Washington, DC 75
Wirsching, Joseph 95
The Woman in White 79

Yogesh xxvi, 52, 56

FILM INDEX

Aag (1948) 12
Aakash Deep (1965) 99, 102
Aakhri Dao (1958) 59
Aakhri Khat (1966) 86–7
Aap ki Parchhaiyan (1964) 63
Aap ki sewa mein (1947) 1
Aashirwad (1968) 44
Aaye Din Bahar Ke (1966) 78
Ab Dilli Door Nahin (1957) 13
Abhinetri (1970) 81
Adalat (1958) 63
Agni Pareeksha (1981) 54
Agni Pariksha (1954) 18
Albela (1951) 51
Albela (1971) 19
Aman (1967) 12, 20
Amrapali (1966) 57
Anamika (1973) 69, 72–3
Anand (1970) 54–5
Anandmath (1952) 84
Anarkali (1953) xv, 46, 50–2, 84, 95
Andaz (1949) 24–5, 42
Andolan (1951) 8
Anita (1967) 76, 79–80
Anmol Ghadi (1946) 104
Annadata (1972) 52, 54–6
Anokhi Raat (1968) 33
Anpadh (1962) 63
Aradhana (1969) 73
Ayee Milan ki bela (1964) 17

Baharon ke Sapne (1967) 69, 71
Bandini (1963) 53
Bari Bahen (1949) 39
Barkha (1957) 100
Barsaat (1949) 12–14, 27, 42, 50
Barsaat ki Raat (1960) xix, 31, 33
Basant Bahar (1956) 11
Bazaar (1982) 86, 89, 91
Bazar (1949) 41
Bees Saal Baad (1962) 84–5
Beti Bete (1964) 11, 17
Bezubaan (1962) 100
Bhairavi (shelved) 32
Bhatruhari (1932) 95
Bobby (1973) 15
Boot Polish (1954) 13
Burmah Road (1962) 100–1
Buzdil (1951) 28

Caravan (1972) 73
Chal Chal re Naujawan (1944) 3
Chand Mere Aja (1960) 100

Chhoti Si Mulaqat (1967) 12, 18, 20
Chitralekha (1964) 32–3
Chori Chori (1956) 28

Dastan (1950) 21
Deya Neya (1963) 22
Dharti Kahe Pukar Ke (1969) 29
Dil ki Rahen (1973) 61
Dillagi (1948) 21
Diwana (1952) 108
Do Aankhen Barah Haath (1957) 44
Do Chor (1972) 30
Dost (1974) 78
Dosti (1964) 63
Dulari (1949) 23

Gajabau (1943) 1
Gazal (1964) 63
Goonj Uthi Shehnai (1959) 44
Guddu (1995) 24
Guest House (1959) 100

Haqueeqat (1964) 61, 64
Hare Rama Hare Krishna (1971) 74
Harishchandra Taramati (1963) 79
Heena (1991) 116
Heera Panna (1973) 70
House number 44 (1955) 28
Hulchul (1951) 57

Ishk Ishk Ishk (1974) 74

Jahan Ara (1964) 63
Jewel Thief (1967) 70
Jhanak Jhanak Payal Baaje (1955) 43–4, 46
Jhanjhar (1953) 52
Jhumroo (1961) 35
Joru ka bhai (1955) 34–5
Julie (1975) 92
Jyoti (1969) 27, 29–30

Khazanchi (1941) 3
Kohinoor (1960) 23
Kohraa (1964) 83–5
Kunwara Baap (1974) 92

Laat Saheb (1967) 32
Ladli (1949) 6, 8
Lahore (1949) 42
Limelight (1952) 30

Madhumati (1958) 54
Mahal (1949) 6, 27, 42, 50
Majboor (1948) 1–2
Malhar (1951) 31, 33
Mashal (1950) 27

Mayurpankh (1954) 13, 16
Mehboob ki Mehndi (1971) 76, 80
Mera Naam Joker (1970) 15
Mera Saaya (1966) 79
Mere Mehboob (1963) 23
Mizra Ghalib (1954) 95
Mother India (1957) 17
Mughal-e-Azam (1960) 104

Naata (1955) 105
Naaz (1954) 15
Nadaan (1971) 19
Nagin (1954) xiv, 46, 84
Naya Din Nai Raat (1974) 78

Oonche Log (1966) 102

Padosan (1968) 5
Pakeezah (1972) 72, 94–5
Parakh (1960) 52, 54–5, 59
Parasmani (1963) 77
Patang (1960) 100
Patrani (1956) 14
Paying Guest (1957) 26
Pooja ke Phool (1964) 63
Poonam (1952) 13
Pushpanjali (1970) 78
Pyaasa (1957) 28
Pyar Kiye Jaa (1966) 78

Raat aur Din (1967) 12, 17–18
Raja aur Runk (1968) 17
Rajkumar (1964) 17
Ram Teri Ganga Maili (1985) 115–16
Razia Sultan (1983) 86
Rebecca (1940) 85
Reshma aur Shera (1971) 34–5
Rustom Sohrab (1963) 58

Samar (1950) 27
Sangam (1964) 17–18, 20
Sangat (1975) 54
Sangdil (1952) 59
Sati Savitri (1964) 79
Satyam Shivam Sundaram (1978) 79
Sau Saal Baad (1966) 81
Seema (1955) 14
Shabab (1954) 25
Shagird (1967) 81
Shaheed (1948) 9, 84
Shankar Husain (1977) 86, 88
Sharabi (1964) 63
Sharada (1957) 16
Shehnai (1957) 51
Shikari (1963) 101
Shirin Farhad (1956) 103, 105
Shola Aur Shabnam (1961) 87

Subah (1982) 108
Suhagan (1964) 63
Surili (unreleased) 51
Swami (1977) 91–2

Taj Mahal (1963) 31, 33
Teesri Manzil (1966) 30, 71
The Hound of the Baskervilles 85
The Train (1970) xv

Udhar ka Sindoor (1976) 92
Ujala (1959) 11, 16
Umbartha (1982) 110

Vertigo (1958) 79

Woh Kaun Thi? (1964) 63, 79–80

Ziddi (1948) 4–5, 9

SONG INDEX

Aaj kal mein dhal gaya 11, 17
Aaj mere naseeb mein 57–8
Aaja re mere pyar ke rahi 102
Aankh se aankh milata hai koi 113
Aap ki nazron ne samjha 63
Aap Yun Faaslon Se 86
Aawara aye mere dil 12, 17
Aayega aane wala 6
Ab tera intezaar kaun kare 34
Ae pyar teri dunia se hum 52
Ai dil-e-nadaan 86
Ai Dilruba nazren mila 58
Apne Aap Raaton Mein 86, 88
Arre jane na dungi 34
Awaaz de kahan hai 104

Baahon Mein Chale Aao 69, 72
Bade armaano se 31, 33
Baharen phir bhi aayegi 42
Baharon Mera Jeevan Bhi Sanwaro 86
Baithe hain kya unke pass 70

Chale jana nahin 39–41
Chand phir nikla 26, 28
Chanda re ja re ja re 4–5
Chhed gayo mohe sapne mein 52
Chilo chaand megher paare 30
Chup chup khade ho zaroor koi baat hai 40

Dagabaaz ho banke piya 100–1
Dekhiye Sahibon 71
Dekhte dekhte jal gaya aasmaan 105
Devta maana aur pooja teri tasveer ko 19
Dikhai Diye Yun 86, 89–91
Dil ka diya jala kar gaya 99, 101
Dil ka khilona hai toot gaya 44
Dil ki girah khol do 18
Dil mera toda 1–2, 5
Do sitaron ka zameen 24–5

Ek Chatur Naar 5
Ek Mithi se Chubhan 34

Gagana sadana 110
Gahan rati ghanay 56
Ghiri ghiri ghatayen aasmaan par 108
Guzra hua zamana aata naheen dobara 103–5

Har ik baat pe 111–12
How do you hold a moonbeam in your hand xi
Husn pahadon ka 115

Ich Liebe dich 20

Ja ri ja nindiya 52
Jaane kyon log mohobbat 76, 80
Jao re jogi tum jao re 57
Jawan Hai Mohobaat 104
Jawani ki rail chali jaye re 51
Jeet hi lenge baazi hum tum 87
Jeevan dor tumhi sang bandhi 79
Jeevan ke do raahen pe khade 12, 19
Jhan jhan jhan jhan payal baaje 28
Jhil mil sitaron ke tale 7–8
Jhir jhir barse sawani ankhiyan 44
Jo dil mein khushi bankar aaye 40
Jurm-e Ulfat pe 31, 33

Kabhi to aa 14
Kahin Deep Jale Kahin Dil 84
Kaise jeete hain bhala 78
Kali palak teri gori 30
Kanha bole na 54
Kar gaya re 13, 16
Kareeb aa yeh nazar 76, 79
Karoge Yaad Toh 91
Khelo na mere dil se 64
Koi humdum na raha 35
Krishna Krishna 78
Kya Jaanu Sajan 69–71

Lag ja gale 63, 80
Limelight theme 30

Main jagun re tu so jaa 44
Marna teri gali mein 25
Meghwa gagan beech jhanke 79
Mehlon ka raja mila 33
Mera naam hai Chameli 17
Mera watan Japan 12, 20–1
Mere Manke Diye 52, 55
Mila hai kisika jhumka 55
Mujhe dard-e-dil ka pata na tha 102
Mujhe mil gaya bahana 31, 33
Mujhse mat pooch 49, 52

Na jeona 55, 59
Nadaan title song 19
Nain so nain nahin milao 43–4, 46
Naina basre 63
Natun phagune jabe 5
Nisdin nisdin 57

O Bekaraar Dil 83–5
O ghata saanwari 81
O mora nadaan balma 11, 16
O re man gungun 54
O sajna 55, 59
Ore maajhi 53

Pal Bhar Mein Yeh Kya Ho Gaya 91–3
Panna ki Tamanna 69, 74
Phaili hui hai sapno ki baahen 28
Prem nagar mein basne walo 13

Raat aur Din title song 18
Raaton ke saaye ghane 52, 56–7
Raghupati Raghav Raja Ram 33
Rasa sayang re 20
Rasik Balma 28
Rasm-e-ulfat 61, 66
Roop tera mastana 73
Rut phire par din hamare 28

Sajan ki galiyan chhod chale 41–3
Sakhi re mera man 32, 34
Sam 93
Sanjh bari ghar aaja re piya 111
Sansaar se bhage phirte ho 34
Satyam Shivam Sundaram title song 79
Sayonara 20
Shaam dhale jamuna kinare 78
Soch ke ye gagan jhoomen 27, 30–1
Sun lo sajan meri baat 42
Sun munne mere 30
Suno chhotisi gudiya ki lambi kahani 14

Taqdeer jaga kar aayi hoon 21, 23, 25
Tere pyaar mein dildaar 24
Thade rahiyo o Banke yaar re 94, 96
Thane kain kain bol sanava 108–9
Tod diya dil mera 25
Tujhe kya sunau main dilruba 59
Tum asha vishwas hamare 108, 110
Tumhare bulane ko 6, 8
Tumi pathor chokheo je drishti 111
Tumko piya dil diya 101
Tumne mujhe dekha 30

Woh hain zara khafa khafa 81
Woh pass rahen ya door rahen 41

Yeh hawa ye raat ye chandni 59
Yeh raat bhi jaa rahi hai 81
Yun hasraton ke daag 63

Zara si aahat hoti hai 62, 64–6